easy
decorating

*Make your home
a haven of comfort and
creativity. We'll show you
how to decorate
every room.*

Oxmoor
House.

editor's note

CHANCES ARE, YOU'RE READY for some new thoughts on decorating. Congratulations! You've come to just the right place. Let *Southern Living At HOME* show you how to achieve a stylish look easily and effectively.

We've pulled together many of our best ideas for rooms that are fresh and individual yet have lasting appeal. Creative home design requires a commitment of time, energy, and resources, so we want you to be delighted with your results.

To kick things off, we present four appealing decorating styles: Cottage, City, Coastal, and Woodland. Then we explore color, fabric, art, and many of the other elements that are the building blocks of a great-looking home. Next, our array of completed rooms demonstrates some simple uses of design components.

Enjoy exploring our easy decorating ideas, and use them to make your home even more beautiful.

Julia Hamilton

Julia Hamilton
Editor

Southern Living
Easy Decorating

SOUTHERN LIVING
EDITOR: Julia Hamilton
ART DIRECTOR: Patricia See Hooten
COPY CHIEF: Dawn P. Cannon
COPY EDITOR: Rhonda Richards
PRODUCTION COORDINATOR: Christy Coleman
HOMES STAFF: Sara Anderson, Alice Welsh Doyle, Robert C. Martin, Amy Bickers Mercer, Julie Feagin Sandner
CONTRIBUTORS: Jean M. Allsopp, Cindy Manning Barr, Sarah Brueggemann, Robbie Caponetto, Alicia K. Clavell, Missie Neville Crawford, Mary Leigh Fitts, Majella Chube Hamilton, Sarah Jernigan, Emily Minton, Allen Rokach, Leslie Byars Simpson, Ann E. Stratton
SENIOR PHOTOGRAPHERS: Ralph Anderson, Van Chaplin, Joseph De Sciose, Art Meripol, John O'Hagan, Mark Sandlin, Charles Walton IV
PHOTOGRAPHERS: Jim Bathie, Gary Clark, Tina Cornett, William Dickey, Beth Dreiling, Laurey W. Glenn, Meg McKinney
ASSISTANT PHOTOGRAPHER: Mary Margaret Chambliss
SENIOR PHOTO STYLIST: Buffy Hargett
PHOTO STYLIST: Rose Nguyen
ASSOCIATE PHOTO STYLIST: Alan Henderson
ASSISTANT PHOTO STYLISTS: Lisa Powell Bailey, Cari South
PHOTO LIBRARIAN: Tracy Duncan
PHOTO PRODUCTION MANAGER: Larry Hunter
PHOTO SERVICES: Amanda Leigh Abbett, Ginny P. Allen, Catherine Carr, Lisa Dawn Love

EDITOR IN CHIEF: John Alex Floyd, Jr.
MANAGING EDITOR: Clay Nordan
EXECUTIVE EDITORS: Derick Belden, Susan Dosier, Warner McGowin, Dianne Young
DEPUTY EDITOR: Kenner Patton
ART DIRECTOR: Craig Smith
PRODUCTION AND COLOR QUALITY MANAGER: Katie Terrell Morrow
CREATIVE DEVELOPMENT DIRECTOR: Valerie Fraser Luesse
PHOTOGRAPHY AND COVER ART DIRECTOR: Jon Thompson
ASSISTANT TO THE EDITOR IN CHIEF: Marian Cooper
OFFICE MANAGER: Wanda T. Stephens
ADMINISTRATIVE ASSISTANTS: Chris Carrier Garmon, Lynne Long, Sandra J. Thomas
EDITORIAL ASSISTANTS: Karen Brechin, Charlotte Liapis, Catherine K. Russell
ASSOCIATE ART DIRECTOR: Claudia Hon
ASSISTANT ART DIRECTOR: Gae Watson
SENIOR DESIGNER: Jennie McClain Shannon
DESIGNER: Amy Kathryn R. Merk
DESIGNER/ILLUSTRATOR: Christopher Davis
ASSISTANT COPY CHIEF: Paula Hughes
SENIOR COPY EDITOR: Julia Pittard Coker
COPY EDITOR: Cindy Riegle
ASSISTANT COPY EDITORS: Katie Bowlby, Leah Dueffer, Stephanie Gibson Mims, Libby Monteith Minor, JoAnn Weatherly
COPY ASSISTANT: Tara Ivey
ASSISTANT PRODUCTION MANAGER: Jamie Barnhart
PRODUCTION COORDINATORS: Paula Dennis, Allison Brooke Krannich

OXMOOR HOUSE, INC.
EDITOR IN CHIEF: Nancy Fitzpatrick Wyatt
EXECUTIVE EDITOR: Susan Carlisle Payne
COPY CHIEF: Allison Long Lowery
EDITOR: Rebecca Brennan
SENIOR DESIGNER: Emily Albright Parrish
COPY EDITOR: Donna Baldone
CONTRIBUTING EDITORIAL ASSISTANT: Laura K. Womble

SOUTHERN LIVING AT HOME®
SENIOR VICE PRESIDENT & EXECUTIVE DIRECTOR: Dianne Mooney
DIRECTOR OF BRAND MANAGEMENT: Gary Wright
DIRECTOR OF DESIGN: Melanie Grant
RESEARCH MANAGER: Jon Williams

SOUTHERN LIVING® EASY DECORATING

ISBN-13: 978-0-8487-3176-2
ISBN-10: 0-8487-3176-x
Printed in the United States of America
First Printing 2007
Southern Living is a registered trademark of Southern Living, Inc., U.S. Patent and Trademark Office.

Created exclusively for *Southern Living At HOME*, the Direct Selling Company of Southern Progress Corporation. For information about *Southern Living At HOME*, please write to: Consultant Support, P.O. Box 830951, Birmingham, AL 35283-0951

on the cover:

Refresh your rooms the easy way—with bold strokes of color such as aqua and turquoise. For more, see "Following Fashion" on page 112.

Photograph: Van Chaplin
Styling: Leslie Byars Simpson

contents

Learn the best tips for decorating your home to reflect your personal style.

for great style 4

using the elements of design 36

ideas for every room 78

for great style

You'll find plenty
of inspiration in this
idea-filled gallery of homes
featuring cottage, city,
coastal, and
woodland styles.

Cottage

Limited space in no
way means limited
style. Just create a
space that's whimsical,
informal, nostalgic,
and totally comfortable.
Collect vintage wooden
furniture, and retain its
original weathered fin-
ish. Choose simple
fabrics, and showcase
found objects. Person-
alize each room for a
collected look that's
never fussy or busy—it
simply says home.

City

Sleek and sophisticated, this style generates a simplicity and energy that's miles away from suburbia. Use bold, bright accents of color, or choose an all-white minimalist look. Utilize the steel, glass, brick, and stone that are characteristic of urban settings. Mix antiques and contemporary art. Whether bold and bright or crisp and chic, the look is sharp, not harsh.

Coastal

Coastal style is as much a frame of mind as it is a particular look. Think of your favorite beach retreat adapted for full-time living. It's casual and comfortable, showing an appreciation for water, sand, and sun. Interiors feature a fresh color palette ranging from neutrals to more vibrant hues. They can't help but say, "Relax, and welcome to the coast!"

Woodland

Either rustic or refined, woodland style is purely a reflection of one's love for and respect of nature. Interiors form a seamless connection to the surrounding views of the outdoors. Accessories are often down-to-earth jars, bottles, baskets, and crafts found locally. Rich colors and a variety of natural textures enhance the lodge-like feeling.

charming
transformation

This appealing yellow unites a variety of spaces created during remodeling. French doors open to the new bluestone terrace.

Thoughtful renovations and cosmetic improvements turned this older house into home sweet home.

Making wise choices, both in expanding the house and in reusing what was already there, owners Marguerita and George Riggall landed the home of their dreams. Although time had been relatively kind to this 1926 English-influenced cottage, it awaited talented homeowners like the Riggalls to resurrect its former charm.

Though previously remodeled, the kitchen lacked the appeal that characterized the rest of the house. "The challenge here was to make the most of the existing space while giving the kitchen a gourmet look with stainless steel fixtures," says Marguerita. The Riggalls renovated the kitchen, choosing to keep it the same size, and now it's one of their favorite areas.

The most significant change was the addition that connects all the main rooms on the first floor. Architect Nancy Hayden of Nashville designed a breakfast room as an extension of the kitchen, and she also provided for a comfortable yet elegant family room. To access the back-yard, ample pairs of 9-foot-tall French doors lead from the family room to the garden beyond.

With smart design choices and creative solutions, the Riggalls have unlocked the potential of their home.

KEYS TO COTTAGE STYLE

Idea #1: Make the most of what you have.

Look for ways to utilize design elements that your home already possesses. Though the Riggalls' kitchen had been previously remodeled, the oversize island hampered traffic flow. Their solution was to reuse and rearrange much of the cabinetry and add a new island to improve circulation.

Idea #2: Add architectural elements.

Working with the existing style of your home, introduce appropriate new features when possible. The Riggalls consulted craftsman/builder Jim Lowe and craftsman Dave DesFosses regarding major improvements, such as the breakfast space that's part of the new addition. Surprisingly, the handsome oval window above the china cabinet is a stock item, costing less than a custom one. It also makes a great focal point within the groin-vaulted ceiling.

Idea #3: Refresh with color.

While you're remodeling, treat yourself to an upbeat new range of colors. With a fresh paint palette, you can emphasize structural improvements while brightening formerly dark spaces. In some of its added and remodeled areas, this welcoming cottage enjoys sunny yellow walls combined with sparkling white trimwork.

above: **As part of the new addition, this area of the breakfast room serves as a great display space for glassware and crystal.**

left: **Topped by a granite countertop, the island is home to a hammered copper vegetable sink and a wine cooler.**

'small cottage,
BIG STYLE

Make your space live large with these simple styling ideas.

SUCCESSFULLY DECORATING A COMPACT HOUSE means finding ways to make your rooms look more spacious. The right furniture helps, as do creative wall arrangements. One of the easiest (and least expensive) tricks is color, color, color. Not big, bold splashes of it, but a sophisticated mix of neutrals— from cream to caramel beige to antique white. Together, these shades can make your surroundings grow before your very eyes. Put these hue clues and other design moves to the test.

KEYS TO COTTAGE STYLE

Idea #1: Remain neutral.

Today's neutrals are anything but bland. Stick with a pale palette for all your main rooms; they'll flow together better and appear larger. Paint shelves, built-ins, and kitchen cabinetry a light, neutral color. If the wood surfaces are the same shade as your walls, they'll blend in and look as if they take up less space. Keep floors neutral, too, with sisal or sea grass rugs bound with a tan or cream trim.

Idea #2: Hang smart wall art.

So you don't have a lot of wallspace? Just get creative with where you put art. In this living room, a picture hangs from the center of the window frame. A gold-leaf mirror, flanked by two architectural pieces of carved and gilded wood, adorns the front of built-in shelving. The backs of the shelves are covered with yellow-and-white-striped wallpaper, adding more color to the mix. Another way to expand a room: Think vertically. Start at eye level, and mount artwork in a column all the way to the ceiling; your eye will travel upward, making the walls feel taller.

Idea #3: Hang those curtains high.

You don't want draperies to overpower compact quarters. Hang them close to the ceiling, and puddle an inch or two of fabric on the floor. Also, make sure the rod extends about a foot beyond each side of the window so that when the curtains are open, the maximum amount of natural light can spill into the room.

Idea #4: Avoid chunky furniture.

Furniture with clean lines and thin legs (notice the coffee table and chairs in the living room) can make rooms look more open and inviting. Purchase lamps with thin bases, and choose demilunes (half tables) with slender legs.

Idea #5: Gleam is a good thing.

Accessories and furniture with shiny surfaces bounce light around your room, visually expanding the space. Opt for a glass coffee table, like the one in this home, or a side table with a beaming marble top. Use mirrors and lamps to brighten dark corners.

HOMEOWNER: RANDY POWERS

above: **To enlarge a room without major remodeling, choose warm neutral shades for walls and furniture, and inject color with accessories. Just as a pinstriped shirt makes a person look taller, panels with vertical stripes add height to a window.** *above, right:* **Glass cabinetry can enlarge a not-so-big kitchen. Wallpaper or paint the back of the shelves for visual interest.**

relaxing retreat

Put together a fresh cottage look with a blend of rustic and refined accents.

AN UPDATED FARMHOUSE THAT'S UNPRETENTIOUS, enchanting, and able to stand up to three boys sums up this house. "The home is only an hour from Atlanta, but I wanted the family to feel like they were going to a whole other place," says designer Shane Meder. Borrow some of his great ideas to create your own cottage in the city or country.

Idea #1: **Choose versatile and fuss-free furnishings.**
Combine washable slipcovers with upholstered pieces in textured fabrics that tend to hide dirt. Use lively tapestry pillows to brighten chairs and sofas. Mix wood pieces in several finishes to bring a richness to rooms. Then add some painted, distressed items as well—a few more scratches won't make a difference.

Idea #2: **Paint walls in light, fresh tones.**
For cottage charm, use shades of cream, pale yellow, or soft blue for the walls. White is also a great choice. "Dark, rich colors would feel out of place in this setting," says Shane. "I chose a

above, left: **Even humble items, such as these old rolling pins, look special when displayed in a collection.**
above: **A pretty painted cabinet in soft colors highlights a wall.**
above, right: **Small plates combined with prints make an informal display.**

summer palette with a very clean feel. I don't think of a sweet child's pastels, but rather muted tones of stronger shades." For example, a faded aqua enlivens the family room, and a buttermilk yellow wraps the living room with subtle warmth. A crisp white serves as the ideal backdrop for the boys' bedroom with its Americana theme. ▶

color tips

Need a paint shade to make your rooms look larger? Here are a few of our favorite neutrals. Try painting trim and walls the same color. Use an eggshell finish for walls and a high-gloss finish for trim.

- Cottage White (KM3985-1) by Kelly-Moore
- Natural Wicker (950) by Benjamin Moore
- Antique White (6119) by Sherwin-Williams
- Oyster (26) by Kelly-Moore
- Swiss Coffee (1812) by Behr
- Navajo White (947) by Benjamin Moore
- Linen White (912) by Benjamin Moore
- Lancaster White (ready-made color) by Benjamin Moore
- Roadster White (WH02A) by Ralph Lauren
- Zurich White (1039) by Sherwin-Williams
- Sleek White (1018) by Sherwin-Williams

Idea #3: Add charming collections in diverse styles.

The goal is to look like you've inherited things from previous generations and have been adding to those collections yourself. Think layered and effortless, not rigid.

Idea #4: Cover walls with art and objects.

"I prefer the art to appear collected, as though acquired over time during one's travels," says Shane. "It makes the interiors look lived in, instead of formal." Objects bring a unique look as well. Hang plates with prints in a living room or vintage cooking utensils with old grocery signs in a kitchen.

Idea #5: Place fresh flowers in simple containers.

Casual flowers bring charm, color, and scent to rooms. Arrange daisies in milk bottles or roses in a white pitcher. Shane puts bunches of rosemary in unpolished silver pitchers. "I know it's a little untraditional to show tarnish, but I love the patina of old, unpolished silver," he says. That's the whole point to this cottage style though—to give tradition a good-natured pinch.

above, left: **Collected treasures displayed atop the mantel live comfortably with artwork hung on the wall.** *top:* **Fresh greenery and flowers find an unexpected home in a pair of silver pitchers.** *above:* **An antique pine bench holds a group of small vases brightened with gerbera daisies.**

creating cottage style

Capturing a COZY LOOK is all about making the most of small spaces, mixing old and new, and playing with color.

You don't have to start from scratch to give your home a casual, cottage feel. Repainting and re-accessorizing can go a long way.

▶ A simple color scheme looks best in compact spaces. The shades can be whatever you want—from bright to subdued—but try to limit them to two or three. Go for neutral tones with a hint of yellow here and there, or use a trio of soft green, cream, and blue.

▶ Comfort is key to pulling off cottage style, and that's where fabrics can enter the scene. Decorate with materials that are soft and cozy, as opposed to those that look like they shouldn't be touched. On furniture, pillows, and curtains, opt for cotton toiles, florals, or stripes.

▶ Don't be afraid to mix older items with contemporary pieces. Candlesticks found at a flea market look great on top of a sleek glass coffee table, for example.

▶ Accent your rooms with natural elements, such as woven blinds and sisal or sea grass rugs. Frame botanical prints to display in entryways, powder rooms, and kitchens. Arrange fresh flowers in everyday containers, including bowls, glass jars, and ceramic pitchers.

FIND YOURSELF A loft

Enjoy open rooms with **city views** at a convenient downtown address.

HOMEOWNERS SEEKING A CHANGE FROM THE SUBURBS are discovering the benefits of loft living. By chance, a brick office building in the heart of Asheville, North Carolina, caught Amy Parker's eye. "Because this place was located in a very hip, fun part of town with lots of art galleries and studios," she says, "I began thinking about the potential of living there as well." Testing her luck, Amy inquired and was delighted to learn that the space was for sale.

left: **This sleek, generous bar frames the kitchen beyond the curvy counter.**
below, left: **Spacious interiors, tall ceilings, contemporary furniture, and an abundance of natural light suit the loft's architectural simplicity.**

What she saw the first time was a floor of numerous small offices that were being used for storage—or not at all. It was anything but the cool, livable loft it is today. Her experience shows how it's possible to convert the most unlikely surroundings into a fabulous home.

Dreaming of open, light-drenched rooms with downtown vistas, Amy relied on architect Wayland Plaster for design help. With contractor Kirk Boone, they accomplished her goal of maintaining an unobstructed flow among the kitchen, bar, and living areas by knocking down walls to open up the space.

Amy used bold red accents to punctuate the seating group in the neutral living area. Adding black granite countertops, maple cabinetry, and slate flooring to the new, sleek kitchen made it the showpiece of the third-floor space. Amy sums it all up by saying, "Renovating this loft space into a beautiful home fits right in with my 21st-century, big-dreaming lifestyle. Plus, I'm in a part of town where I feel right at home."

KEYS TO CITY STYLE

Idea #1: Make it your own.

Think of a loft as a blank canvas, presenting nearly endless opportunities to determine your own design direction. Loft space is generally quite flexible in that it can be finished as elegant, cozy, or industrial as you desire.

Idea #2: Work with existing materials.

Make existing air ducts, returns, and other functional elements a feature of the loft's design. They can enhance the urban feel. Or, as a means of camouflage, you can paint them the same color as surrounding walls and ceilings. Consider other characteristics, such as existing brick walls and architectural details, as part of the space's charm. The terrific pressed-tin ceiling panels throughout Amy's loft are an original feature.

Idea #3: Keep it simple.

Streamlined, contemporary furnishings are a natural accompaniment with big-scale city spaces. A loft is the ideal setting to indulge in sculptural sofas and chairs with lots of personality and pizzazz. In the wide-open rooms, they can easily be viewed (and admired) from each side. Limit accessories to avoid a cluttered look. Incorporate hidden storage wherever possible, or let built-ins showcase everyday items. Here, a custom wine rack and bookcases serve both artful and practical purposes.

top: **The kitchen's full ceiling of glass panels and steel framing illuminates the cooking space. Maple cabinets echo the light color of the wood floors in other areas.** *above:* **Amy's banquette is conveniently tucked into a corner of the kitchen.**

Antiques and carefully chosen accents stand out against a neutral color palette. Resting in a sunny spot on the ottoman, an antique jar holds a bountiful bouquet.

EXPLORE THE WORLD OF design

Soft colors and minimal accessories present a fresh take on city style.

nEUTRALS AND AGED PATINAS REIGN COMFORTABLY in this sophisticated and eclectic Dallas home. Shannon and Andrew Newsom sprinkle each room with their delightful finds, including one-of-a-kind objects and fabulous furniture pieces that would work well in any setting. Sideboards and tables hold all manner of collectibles the couple has grown to love.

As owners of *Wisteria,* a catalog of home and garden furnishings, the Newsoms travel the world in search of objects for its pages. "Our style tends toward a minimalist and informal look," says Shannon, "but we also appreciate antiques and fine decorative items." On frequent trips, the couple acquires special pieces for their own collections, and sometimes they even bring catalog samples home to test-drive for a while. Now that's great customer service.

KEYS TO CITY STYLE

Idea #1: Work with neutrals.

Accent your room with whites, grays, and a host of feel-good fabrics. In the Newsoms' living room, slipcovers dress already-comfortable furnishings. "All-white and linen fabrics can be intimidating," says Shannon, "but I like them because they're surprisingly easy to launder."

▶

HOMEOWNERS: SHANNON AND ANDREW NEWSOM

Idea #2: Include antiques and vintage pieces.

Add richness to understated surroundings with timeworn woods and layered paint finishes. Cover pillows with fragments of old fabrics and needlework. In the Newsoms' dining room, a 17th-century Spanish table mixes with nail-trimmed French chairs, while a seasoned buffet holds an arrangement of tall candlesticks and various containers.

Idea #3: Accessorize mostly in black and white.

Choose accessories that are subdued in color so that you can easily move them from room to room. Shannon and Andrew collect handmade containers, storage pots, black-and-white prints, and religious figures to flavor their interiors. To keep things fresh, they occasionally introduce accents of brighter hues.

Idea #4: Include organic elements.

Give life to your rooms with fresh greenery and other natural elements. Include fabrics and art containing images of flowers and foliage. The couple uses their well-loved antique tapestry chairs to flank a series of old botanical prints, and they fill containers throughout with budding bulbs and fresh blossoms.

top: **With its Spanish table and French chairs, the dining room recalls the Newsoms' travels and diverse interests.** *above:* **"This vignette reflects our interest in nature and gardening," says Shannon. "It also points to the overall style and theme of the house."**

creating city style

When you're headed DOWNTOWN with your decorating, here's how to achieve a great new look.

Borrow some of these ideas to fashion your own version of city chic and urban sophistication.

▶ White and off-white walls are hard to beat when you're aiming for a gallery-like setting. They create a clean background for contemporary furniture in bold hues. To showcase antiques and collected treasures from the capitals of the world, opt for ivory and vanilla wall surfaces instead of stark white.

▶ Brightly colored furniture really packs a punch in a loft-like setting. Consider including some leather pieces—they're comfortable, durable, and available in many hues. If you're taking the antiques route, look for old chair frames with distressed or painted wood. They look terrific when redone with natural-fiber fabric seats.

▶ Your favorite accessories will have more opportunity to shine when given plenty of space. Coordinate the look of your lamps, dinnerware, candlesticks—even your wine goblets—with your design. Mix materials, balancing glass with iron and playing porcelain against stone.

tropical touches

above: **Mix striking upholstered pieces with traditional accents.** *right:* **Don't overdo a bold print. In an adjoining seating area, four chairs sport a subdued check for a soft look against the palm-print window treatments.**

This elegant look mingles the colors of the nearby marshes with exotic accents and French furnishings.

COLORS OF COASTAL LIFE INSPIRE MANY IDEAS. There's the beach and blue sky and then there's the green side—tropical plants and native grasses. For this house, the lush marshes of Georgia's coast sparked the color palette. Soft greens, golds, and browns combine for a soothing and polished look that's at home anywhere.

KEYS TO COASTAL STYLE

Idea #1: Put together a sophisticated tropical play.

You can be exotic without being loud. Here, a standout fabric with palm trees, pineapples, and pomegranates brings an island touch to an elegant cocoa brown background. Designer Lori Cook used this pattern for a French chair and window treatments. "It reflects the colors of the marsh that you see across the street," says Lori. "I didn't want the interiors to compete with that beautiful view." Above the mantel hangs a scene of another marsh with a prominent palm tree, and on an opposite wall, palm tree prints with dark frames look fresh when placed together and stacked. You can also bring in plants to fill voids and add life to a space.

Idea #2: Add unexpected touches.

A room that's too thematic risks being either boring or kitschy. That's why you want to add a few unexpected items. A large, skirted ottoman sports an animal motif in chocolate and cream. Sea grass is often used in coastal homes, but a soft Aubusson rug in muted colors anchors this living room. It's also a practical choice for this family, which includes many young grandchildren. "Natural fiber rugs tend to curl up on the ends over time and can be a tripping hazard," notes Lori.

Idea #3: Combine different furniture finishes.

Forget the idea that everything needs to match. When choosing furniture, mix styles and finishes to create a room that looks collected over time. The changing finishes also draw the eye around the room—a cabinet with a painted ivory finish on one wall and a maple wooden chest on another. There's more variation with the table styles as well—a painted metal coffee table and a rattan-topped table, both with iron legs, and a wooden end table. All are lightweight and can be moved easily if needed. The mantel's natural finish lends a rustic touch in an otherwise elegant room.

HOMEOWNERS: BETTY AND MILLS RENDELL

aubusson rugs

This type of rug was originally produced in the French village of Aubusson in the 17th century. Weavers use a technique that involves interlacing the carpets using a thick thread weave on large looms to create a flat tapestry with no pile. Most Aubusson rugs have soft, delicate colors that feature detailed floral and architectural designs. They are still produced today in India and Asia. (See "Where to Find It" on page 110.)

Pair a cheerful **red**, white, and **blue**
color scheme with classic beach motifs
for a relaxed and fresh look.

capture the
coastal
spirit

below: **Blue checks, red stripes, flags, and shells give this living room loads of personality.**

above: **Red chairs and a wonderful red clock, distressed to look old, take center stage in the dining room. Barstools offer additional seating at the counter.**

INFUSE YOUR HOME WITH SHELLS and other nautical details placed against a background of classic red, white, and blue. It's a beach look that's fun and approachable; nothing is too complicated or serious. "You feel as if you can sit down and put your feet up," says Julia Crye, who decorated the home with her mother, Sally Smith. Keep that sentiment in mind when capturing your own bit of the casual coastal life.

KEYS TO COASTAL STYLE

Idea #1: Start with white walls.

Use white walls and trim to tie your rooms together and to provide a neutral backdrop for colorful artwork and decorative mirrors. While red and blue are important players, white pops up everywhere to reinforce the fresh look. The living room sports a white slipcovered sofa and inexpensive Roman shades. Loose, white-toned shells and starfish sit on wood furniture. ▶

above: **A mirrored porthole over the bed hints at a nautical theme.** *left:* **Shells, displayed alone or on accessories, are a recurring motif throughout the house.** *below, left:* **Glue shells to a simple console table to take it from basic to beachy.**

Idea #2: Choose unique furniture for focal points.

Give each of your rooms a star attraction. A faded blue armoire and red clock draw the eye into the living and dining rooms (shown on pages 22-23). Both look antique, but they're new and only distressed to look that way. "I didn't want to put precious furnishings in the house and have to worry," says Sally. Repeating the theme with different motifs, one small bedroom features a bright red bed frame with boats on the headboard, while another is outfitted with a huge porthole mirror over the bed.

Idea #3: Mix fun patterns.

Select fabrics with American spirit. In the living room, red-and-white stripes combine with a bold blue-and-white check. Accent pillows in varying stripes, checks, and flag patterns sit on all the upholstered furniture, and a bright quilt fabric tops the kitchen counter barstools. In the bedrooms, a faded blue-and-white checkerboard print and a simple patchwork quilt cover the beds, lending a serene atmosphere.

above: **A playful mix of sailboats, used as decorative accents on a bright red headboard and around the room, adds coastal flair.** *right:* **Duplicate this decorator look by gluing found seashells to a favorite mirror.**

Idea #4: Select beach-inspired accessories.

Choose interesting and unexpected pieces that work with your theme and capture everyone's attention. The key to using a motif is not to overdo it, but still have enough to make a statement. In this cottage, Julia says, "We went as beach as we could." Starfish and shells pop up throughout the house, and shells accent a variety of pieces—lamps, a mirror, and a small console table. Large corals and conchs rest atop the blue armoire (page 22). Sailboats float on several surfaces as well.

Idea #5: Opt for fuss-free floors.

Wood floors offer a natural look and are easy to clean and maintain. Use rugs to anchor a seating area or to delineate an open space. Leave the wood floors mostly exposed, and accent with sea grass rugs or other natural fibers such as coir and sisal. If you don't like the feel of these materials under bare feet, then use a solid beige, ivory, or white chenille rug instead. Thick Oriental rugs or plush carpet would look too heavy with this decor.

our favorite sources for
natural-fiber rugs

Pottery Barn
www.potterybarn.com

Crate & Barrel
www.crateandbarrel.com

Sisal Rugs Direct
www.sisalrugs.com

Restoration Hardware
www.restorationhardware.com

cool
comfort

Try these **coastal-inspired ideas,** whether you live at the beach or just want to feel like you do.

Solid-colored furniture lends a simple, relaxed style to the living room. Amber-stained heart-pine floors and a brown leather ottoman add deep, rich color.

JUST BECAUSE YOU LOVE THE BEACH doesn't mean you love beach-theme decorating. You might adore tropical fish, but not when they're a print on your wallpaper. No problem. Pulling off a sophisticated seaside style is not only possible, it's easier than you may think. Take a look inside this home for inspiring ideas. We think you'll like what you see. And there's not a fish motif in sight!

KEYS TO COASTAL STYLE

Idea #1: Pick a refreshing palette.

Bright colors are fun for your beach bag, but if you'd rather not be surrounded by them all day every day, go with calmer, cooler hues. Think of a scheme that an artist would use to paint an ocean scene. Put together paint chips of soft teal, mossy green, blue-gray, oyster white, sandy beige, and coral. Then take your color file with you when you're shopping for furniture, art, curtains, pillows, and accessories.

Idea #2: The brighter the better.

There are many inexpensive ways to bring more light into your home. Leave the windows unadorned or hang white, semi-sheer panels. You could frost windows for additional privacy in a powder room, bath, or bedroom. Another trick: Use large mirrors to reflect light around your home. The best place to hang or prop one is opposite a window so that it can invite another splendid outdoor view into the house.

Idea #3: Think globally.

Many Web sites and furniture stores offer coastal pieces and accessories inspired by styles from Bali to Bermuda. In this living room, a West Indies-style sofa boasts ratcheted arms that fold down, turning the couch into an extra sleeper. Pineapples cap the headboards of twin beds in a guest bedroom. Consider a Balinese-style bench or rug. Buy bamboo blinds for your windows. Toss a Mexican striped throw over a wicker chair. ▶

top: **Furniture is low and set away from unadorned windows so as not to obstruct the view or block sunlight.** *above:* **Use symmetry for stylish arrangements. Note how the trio of potted plants mirrors the three jars of shells and starfish on a shelf below. A pair of floor lamps highlights it all.**

A simple, snowy quilt and satiny linens with bamboo brocade dress a queen-size sleigh bed. A mirror above the headboard reflects a serene outdoor view.

Idea #4: Add touches of pattern.

Subtlety is key here. Place a cluster of tropical-print pillows on a solid-colored sofa. Top a dining room table with leaf-motif place mats or napkins. Or take a cue from this living room, and lay a rug with beach towel-like stripes over hardwood floors.

Idea #5: Put nature on display.

Scatter a few eye-catching pieces here and there. Use coral and puffy sand dollars to fill trays on a bedside table. Fill frames with botanical and bird prints from flea markets or art stores. Embellish the edges of your sheer curtains with dainty seashell trim. On surfaces throughout your house—from the coffee table to a buffet—arrange tropical leaves in glass cylinders and small bud vases, or anchor pillar candles in jars filled with sand or river rocks.

A watery gray color on the kitchen walls and ceiling mimics decades-old whitewashed limestone.

creating coastal style

Put together a BREEZY LOOK *that will shine in your home—with or without a beach.*

To experience the flavor of the seashore year-round, try some of these simple ideas.

▶ Choose wall colors that are soothing and refreshing. Think of light, natural tones such as grassy green, soft coral, honey gold, and all shades of white.

▶ Let the light in. Keep windows bare, or use fuss-free classic panels in sheer fabrics, linen, or a favorite print. A white cotton Roman shade offers privacy when needed.

▶ Include tropical touches in your home—framed prints of palm trees, exotic houseplants, and decorative fabrics with bamboo, palm trees, or vibrant flowers. Or go with the beach motif, and place shells, starfish, sand dollars, and coral on surfaces around the house. Then add some shell-adorned pieces such as lamps and mirrors.

▶ Use simple floor coverings including natural fiber rugs of sea grass or sisal. Show lots of bare wood, brick, or stone. If you opt for a patterned rug, choose one in muted colors.

red barn escape

A **woodland getaway** showcases the best of worn materials and natural assets.

n NESTLED AMONG TOWERING TREES in a hollow, this board-and-batten cedar barn is both rustic and modern. Its subtle red exterior only hints at the inspired interior.

The Monteagle, Tennessee, getaway of James and Diane Mulloy offers a lesson in balancing primitive elements with spare, contemporary details. Industrial materials add a splash of forward thinking to the timeless decor.

KEYS TO WOODLAND STYLE

Idea #1: Allow nature to inspire you.

Take down heavy curtains or shutters to provide an almost seamless connection between the interior and the land. The lack of window treatments is essential to allow natural light and spectacular views.

Idea #2: Recycle and renew.

Use recycled materials to impart timeworn style. Here, salvaged beams are used for the floorboards, the long dining table, and both fireplace mantels. Re-create a distressed look simply and inexpensively by hitting thick wood with a hammer or a length of chain.

Floor-to-ceiling windows bring the outdoors in and create a tree house-like view from the second level. *above, left:* **Accessories, such as twig-like candle holders, outdoor lighting fixtures, and leather-and-wood barstools, enhance the rustic theme.**

Honed granite, a matte-finish alternative to polished granite, pairs beautifully with distressed red cabinetry.

Idea #3: Bring the outdoors in.

Shop for your indoor decor in the outdoor section of a home-improvement store. Metal exterior light fixtures suspended throughout this cabin maintain a rugged flair. Matching dry-stacked stone chimneys flank the main area.

Idea #4: Add vintage character.

Choose new materials that promote a sense of age. Avoid glossy, slick finishes. Honed granite countertops offer the strength of natural stone. Mimic the look of the distressed red cabinets with matte-finish paint; lightly sand the surface to create spots of wear and tear.

Idea #5: Find beauty in function.

Accessorize your rural retreat with unsophisticated items. Create a simple, practical vignette of walking sticks in an entryway. Use functional and decorative white enamelware in the kitchen.

mountain LODGE

Use hand-hewn materials and a rich palette to adapt your home to rustic surroundings.

NATURAL MATERIALS and warm colors seamlessly blend this cozy hideaway with the surrounding wooded hillsides. Owners Virginia and Bill Spencer planned the main gathering area to contain the kitchen, dining, and living spaces, along with a built-in wet bar. This large room soars skyward in a symphony of beams and planked ceilings, all made from clear white pine. The floors are walnut.

Wanting to maintain the natural, verdant

theme of the place, Bill and Virginia consulted designer Jane Hodges of Birmingham. Her furniture and accessory selections all beautifully complement the house's rustic character.

Many of the furniture pieces in these rooms are handmade. Bill says, "In the creation of this house, Virginia and I used as many local materials and craftsmen as we could." He adds, "I think, above all, that's what makes this place so special." ▶

left: **Vaulted ceilings cap the sun-bathed gathering space.** *above:* **The wide stone fireplace commands attention. Two large, natural arrangements and a wooden deer head balance the space.**

KEYS TO WOODLAND STYLE

Idea #1: ## Open windows to views.

If you're planning to build in a scenic spot, work with a builder and/or architect to ensure that as many rooms as possible will capture the views. The Spencers used French doors and walls of windows to link their living areas to the outdoors.

Idea #2: ## Relax by the fire.

For comfortable, lodge-style living, position the fireplace so that it's the dominant feature of your main living space. Situated opposite a deep sofa, the Spencers' tufted red leather wing chairs invite relaxation by the stone fireplace. A carved wooden deer head above the mantel, feather arrangements, and rustic jugs are just a few of the decorative objects that bring touches of nature indoors.

Idea #3: ## Provide plenty of built-ins.

Stay well-organized with cabinetwork that provides convenient storage space. Two pine storage units flank the handsome stone fireplace. One serves as the entertainment center, and the other consists of open shelves with base cabinets. Adjacent to the living area is a convenient inset bar accented with miniature wooden stag heads similar to the larger one above the mantel. Native materials, such as the twigs that are used as drawer pulls on the bar, accent the rustic character of the house.

Idea #4: ## Keep the kitchen casual.

Even this kitchen is not far removed from the outdoors. The wooden cabinets are forest green, and the countertops (also of wood) are lightly stained. When help-yourself meals are in order, an ample island, along with a useful side counter, provides plenty of serving space. Extra chairs offer seating for a quick snack or room for keeping the cook company. Another convenient feature is the green open cupboard, which stores and displays some of the couple's favorite dishware.

top: **An island provides more seating and work space.**
above: **A farmer's sink and hand towels hung as cafe curtains give this kitchen a casual, down-home feel. The green kitchen cabinetry matches the home's exterior.**

creating woodland style

Try these ideas for creating your own RUSTIC and RELAXED home.

You don't need a mountaintop to create a private retreat. Here are some ways to achieve this comfortable look.

▶ Shop for accent furniture constructed from vines, branches, bamboo, and other natural materials. Look in your own backyard for pinecones, nuts, dried pods, stones, and feathers to use in arrangements. Especially when company is coming, decorate your home with leaves, vegetables, and flowering plants associated with the current season.

▶ Consider the colors of your own natural surroundings when picking fabrics or paints. Rusts, reds, browns, golds, greens, and blues will all remind you of azure skies and splendid treetop views. For informality, use fabrics with simple patterns and uncomplicated textures. Consider staining, instead of painting, interior wooden surfaces. Collect vintage watering cans and metal containers to display on shelves.

▶ Use handmade items, such as one-of-a-kind lamps fashioned from ironstone jars or baskets woven from willow branches. Simple accessories, such as colorful local pottery, wooden bowls, twig serving trays, and rough-hewn candlesticks, will add a casual flair to your interiors.

using the
elements
of design

Reflect your **personal sense of style** in the fabric, furniture, lamps, art, and accessories that you call your own.

WE ALL KNOW A FABULOUS room when we see it. Typically, it's warm and welcoming, harmonious in color, and accented with the owner's treasures. Yet decorating a space can be quite a challenge, especially when you know that even the simplest rooms have many components and involve decision after decision. That's why we're here—to show you some shortcuts and, with the help of many of our favorite homeowners, designers, and architects, to simplify the process of bringing a great room to life.

We'll explain our slant on choosing and using fabrics. You'll discover easy methods for basing a whole room's colors on a catchy piece of artwork or fabric. Sofas and chairs are major purchases, but with tips from a talented designer, you can easily zero in on the right ones. We'll share our thoughts on slipcovers, lamps, artwork, mirrors, window treatments, and much more.

All the elements of design are yours to mix, match, and explore in your own imaginative way. Let's get started.

decorating with
velvet and linen

velvet is a plush, dense fabric that comes in various weights, depending on whether it's used for upholstery or draperies.

Specifics: Velvet imparts warmth and brings a luxurious feel to any room. If velvet upholstery or draperies are too pricey, add some velvet pillows with trim, or try a velvet table skirt or runner.

Take note: Make sure the pile on each piece of velvet runs in the same direction, because the way the light falls on the pile will greatly affect the color.

linen, a natural fiber, is durable and practical, although it does crease and wrinkle easily.

Specifics: Linen hangs well, so use it for window treatments. It also works for upholstery, but it's not as durable as chenille or a heavy woven fabric, so carefully consider its placement.

Take note: Faded-print linens give a new piece of furniture more of an antique quality; bolder print linens tend to take over a small room.

decorating with chenille,
silk, and printed cotton

chenille is made from yarn that has a looped pile, creating a look that is soft and velvet-like.

Specifics: Ideal for upholstery in a family room, it's very durable because the textured finish doesn't show marks as easily as a flat fabric does.

Take note: A good-quality chenille can be pricey, but it's a worthwhile investment for a much-used piece.

silk, made from the filaments of silkworm cocoons, is desired for its wonderful sheen and luxurious look.

Specifics: Use lightweight silk for window treatments and tablecloths. Select slightly heavier silks for little-used decorative upholstery.

Take note: It fades in direct sunlight, so line draperies.

printed cottons are versatile fabrics that can be used for draperies, bedding, and tabletop items.

Specifics: For upholstery, it's not as durable as heavier woven fabrics. Prints work just about anywhere, on their own or as linings for window or bed draperies.

Take note: With large-scale prints, make sure the window or piece of furniture is generous enough to show off the complete pattern.

fabric
know-how
Follow these tips to

From left: **A rich gold velvet with a solid sage green linen and muted floral print linen**

From left: **A cream chenille with a solid pale green silk, cream-and-green striped silk, and a muted cotton print**

decorating with moiré, textured weaves, and damask

moiré, with its slightly ribbed finish, has a watery look from being pressed through engraved rollers.
Specifics: Moiré comes in silk or an acetate-silk blend. Use it for draperies and upholstery. Striped moiré looks great on formal furniture; plaid moirés are more casual.
Take note: Many solid moirés make wonderful linings for window treatments, adding another layer of color.

textured weaves come in all weights, which will determine where you use them.
Specifics: Some weaves have a quilted look that makes them ideal for bedding and upholstery. Those with some man-made fibers are more durable.
Take note: Patterned weaves wear better than plain ones, as marks tend to blend in more with the pattern.

damask is actually a weaving technique that results in a reversible fabric. The most common motifs are scroll and floral designs.
Specifics: Use a satiny-finish damask on furniture for a formal look or cotton damask for everyday pieces.
Take note: Damasks are fairly durable, but avoid delicate silks for upholstery.

decorating with brocades and sheer fabrics

brocade is an expensive, beautiful, woven silk fabric that results from a complicated weaving process using many colors.
Specifics: It has a wonderful sheen and texture. Reserve it for special antique pieces or for pillows to bring a luxe feel to chairs and sofas.
Take note: Brocade will make a reproduction piece look more like an antique.

sheer fabrics can be made of silk, cotton, synthetic fibers, or blends.
Specifics: Ideal for softening a window either paired with drapery panels or alone, sheer fabrics mask an unattractive view or create a sense of privacy while still letting in light. Sheer fabrics make pretty overlays on skirted tables. They also look beautiful as curtains on four-poster beds or simply hanging over a bed.
Take note: Embroidered sheer fabrics bring additional texture and visual interest.

For more information about fabrics: Read *Classic Fabrics* by Henrietta Spencer-Churchill (Rizzoli International Publications, Inc., 1996).

---

learn about fabrics and how to use them with stunning success.

From left: **A plaid moiré, multicolored textured fabric, and a gold damask**

From left: **A pink-toned silk stripe, green-and-pink brocade, and a plaid sheer silk**

pretty fabrics, great ideas

Make any room a study in chic by using fabric in fresh ways everywhere.

YOU'LL LOVE the attention-grabbing ideas that drapery designer Caterina Meadows put into action for her own dining room. "I don't like everything to match," says Caterina. "I like to try unexpected mixes and styles." Her bold room of chocolate brown and chartreuse is not for the timid, but you can apply her expertise to any color palette in any room. Start with luxurious fabrics that feature colors and prints that you love.

Plaids, solids, and prints work together because they all have shades of chocolate brown and chartreuse.

Give a table a designer look. ▶

Caterina's table—made of plywood and topped with a glass round—is actually quite inexpensive. You'd never know that because the beautiful table skirt makes it so fabulous. The design combines a quilted brown velvet top trimmed with tassel fringe and a plaid silk underskirt. You don't have to use silk; other fabrics would work—cotton, linen, or even humble burlap. Translate this same look on a smaller scale for a bedside table or side table in a living room.

Update dining room chairs with new upholstery. ▶

Dining room chairs with upholstered seats are easy to make over with new fabrics. Instead of a plain cover, check out this tufted look. Caterina saw a similar treatment on very expensive chairs in a design magazine, but it translated to her lightweight garden-style chairs. "Usually you see just a few buttons on a tufted chair. This one has 36 for more visual pop," she says. All that tufting takes a little more fabric, but the result is well worth it.

Hang window treatments in a fresh way. ▶

Floor-to-ceiling window treatments will add drama to any room, especially when they're made of silk. Caterina found this silk on the clearance table at a retail fabric store. "It was pretty loud," she says. "I think people were afraid of it, but I could see how beautiful it would be as draperies." Elegant valances, lined in chocolate brown with tassel fringe, add a glamorous note to the panels. Instead of curtain rods, the valances are looped over three square knobs bringing another eye-catching design element into the room.

Think creatively about slipcovers. ▶

Slipcovers are one of decorating's smartest discoveries—their transforming power is enormous. When planning a slipcover, consider using more than one fabric on your chair. Caterina paired a textured burlap-like fabric with leftover silk from the table skirt. "You hate to throw away even a scrap of silk, so I try to use every bit," she explains. The silk runs up the side of the chair, makes up the piping (welt) along the seams, and peeks out from under the skirt like a petticoat. Just a touch of this fine fabric brings a couture attitude to any slipcover.

Use leftover fabric for fabulous pillows. ▶

When shopping for fabric, check out remnants. You may find a small amount of a luxurious fabric that complements your color palette, even if it's just enough for the front of a pillow, the side of a cushion, or a small stool. Caterina's foyer showcases an eclectic blend of pillows on an old church pew. She gave them more oomph with fluffy trims. The seat cushion features the same plaid found in the dining room, dressed up here with a sassy ruffle. Pillows are easy to change out when you want to update a room without spending a lot.

HOMEOWNER: CATERINA MEADOWS

pull color from fabric

Choose a stylish print that makes pulling a room together easy.

instead of heading to the paint store when choosing a color palette, check out your favorite fabric shop. All it takes is a single fabulous print, and you're on your way to a wonderful room without any stress.

1 Create a unified look using one primary fabric.

Don't shy away from a large-scale pattern. A coral-and-cream toile caught designer Lori Cook's eye when she was putting together a sitting area and kitchen for Betty and Mills Rendell. "It's a very distinctive pattern with scenes from Egypt, so I decided to keep it the central design element," says Lori. The toile makes up the cushions on a French armchair and stool as well as window treatments and pillows. A luxurious coordinating tassel trim adorns the pillows and dresses up the simple panels.

Add rich-toned wooden furniture for another layer of subtle color. Let a favorite collection, here ceramic roosters, inspire creative displays as shown on this hutch.

above: **Keep accent fabrics in the same color palette as your base fabric.** *left*: **A large-scale toile sparks the design choices in this sitting area.**

2 Use matching, but not identical, fabrics for other furniture.

Make decisions simple by using only the hues from your starring fabric for the rest of the upholstery. Here the sofa wears a deep coral and the armchair a light cream. A large check in the same tones adds understated pattern to the sofa.

3 Choose a paint color that coordinates with the fabric.

The walls are painted in a neutral color with warm undertones, bringing a sense of unity to the entire room. (See "Where to Find It" on page 110 for paint color.)

4 Add accent pieces to spice up the color palette.

"Use black as a neutral," says Lori. "It works well with almost any color scheme." She chose a tray-style cocktail table, a wood chest that looks like bamboo, and a tole console table as the black accents for the sitting area. The furniture also draws your eye to the Mexican tile floor painted in shades of black and coral. A rooster motif keeps the room lively. A vivid barnyard painting sits atop the black chest, and a collection of roosters nests on the hutch. They even inspired pantry doors painted with country elements, including a basket, pitcher, and wooden candlesticks, all behind chicken wire. The roosters bring a casual note to the room designed for family meals and gatherings. "The toile could go rather formal," says Lori. "The color and whimsy of the roosters keep it grounded."

Find the Right Piece

Whether you're after an original painting or a less expensive option such as a print, be sure you love it. Most retailers or galleries will allow you to take the artwork home on approval. Hang it on a wall to see how you like it. If it doesn't work, return the piece and try again until you find the right one.

Color Quest

Next pick a paint color. Be sure that the shade allows the artwork to stand out—not blend in. In this room, the landscape is made up of green and blue tones with accents of red and yellow. Here, the warm yellow hue on the walls provides an ideal backdrop for the oversize painting.

Furniture Focus

Even the *Mona Lisa* won't look right in a room without proper furniture. Select smart pieces. The rich green chenille sofa is an excellent choice. It's not only comfortable but also has a tall back to anchor the room and to balance the large painting hanging above. Repeating the green color makes this wall a focal point.

Don't get carried away by matching all your furniture to your artwork however. A chocolate velvet library chair offers a neutral accent. Its details, such as exposed wood arms and legs as well as a tufted back, give the room even more character.

Feel free to have a little fun with fabric on smaller pieces of furniture. Try an animal print on an ottoman. Use patterned fabrics on items you can change easily with little expense.

See how
easy it can be
to design
a room around a
favorite painting.

pick colors from art

EVEN A NOTEBOOK of pages from your favorite decorating magazines can leave you wondering where to begin on your next room makeover. Try this idea: Choose a favorite painting or print that will become the focal point of the room. Then pull your color cues for other items from that piece. Yes, it can be that simple. Here's how.

Place a table covered with a patterned, floor-length skirt between solid seating pieces.

HOMEOWNERS: BARBIE AND STEVE COBB

Festive Fabrics

An accent fabric can really complete a room. However, avoid the matching syndrome. Your furniture pieces should coordinate—but not look as if they came as a set. The vibrant red botanical fabric plays off the painting, pulling the room together. The burst of color brightens the dark sofa. It's also used on a table skirt, where you get to see the beauty of the pattern in its entirety.

Defining Details

From lampshades to decorative trim on pillows, details count. A group of majolica plates surround the large painting, giving it even more presence.

Use your creativity when it comes to embellishing pillows. Here, pleated French-blue ribbon makes a cost-effective accent on the animal print pillow.

Two inexpensive fringes are sewn together to create a lush looking trim on the red botanical pillows. The

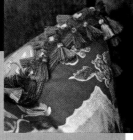

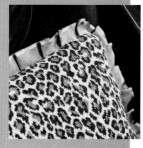

above: **Mix original artwork with reproduction prints. Here, a pair of botanicals hung above the mantel balances the large painting above the sofa. Look for furniture with unique details.** *right:* **Add interesting pillows to solid upholstery fabric. Combine two inexpensive fringes for a truly custom trim on a pillow. Then add a fun print to the mix.**

combination unites all the colors of the room.

It can be so simple to decorate like a professional. Select a favorite painting for your design scheme. Use solid fabrics on large pieces, and then add personality with pillows and accents.

how to buy
a sofa or chair

Get a little expert advice before making that next big upholstery purchase.

SEARCHING FOR THE PERFECT SEATING pieces can be overwhelming. With so many stores and styles, your options seem limitless, and you may not know where to begin. We asked someone known for smart furniture choices to give us some insider tips. Richard Tubb of Birmingham owns a design firm and showroom and has been in the business for more than 32 years.

Stores with small vignettes can help you visualize what the furniture may look like in your home.

RICHARD TUBB INTERIORS, BIRMINGHAM

Q: What if I need furniture for several rooms?
A: Concentrate on one area at a time. Aim for purchasing major items, such as a sofa and chairs, in solid fabrics and smaller elements, such as pillows and throws, in prints. It is much easier and less expensive to change accent pieces rather than your furniture.

Q: How much can I expect to pay?
A: This varies. Count on at least $1,500 for a basic sofa and $850 for a simple club chair. If you purchase for less, the piece probably will not hold up or be a good look. Ask the salesperson about the construction. Low-end frames are usually made from pine or other soft woods and are stapled together. High-end furniture is made from hardwoods that are glued together with dowels and reinforcing corner blocks. They also incorporate a coil system. This is held in place by an eight-way tie of resin-coated twine and then covered in burlap and padding materials.

Q: What are some details I should look for in a sofa or chair?
A: Think classic style. Avoid trendy looks—they change so rapidly. If you choose a piece with a skirt, you may want to go with a waterfall style. This updated look features an attractive skirt that falls from the bottom of the seat cushion.

Q: Should I select down cushions or ones made from a blend?
A: Down cushions are very plush. While that's cozy, every time you stand up you'll have to plump up the pillows. Opt for a polyester/down blend. You'll have the softness of down without losing the structure. Plus you'll have extra cash in your wallet.

Q: What if I see a style I like in a catalog, not on the floor?
A: It's never a good idea to order a sofa or chair from a picture. If the store you're in doesn't carry that model, check with other retailers in the area.

Q: What if I like a style on the floor, but I want to tweak it a bit?
A: Most manufacturers allow special orders. Options, such as a different finish on the legs, the addition of a skirt, and fringes on pillows can be added—most with only a minimal extra charge to the customer.

Q: When can I expect delivery?
A: If you purchase an item off the floor, you can usually get it in a day or so, or you may want to pick it up yourself. However, special orders usually take 8 to 10 weeks. Be sure to check with your salesperson to verify the time frame. Some manufacturers offer a quick-ship program. You pick from a limited selection of fabrics, and it's ready in two weeks.

Q: What if I don't like it after it arrives?
A: Unfortunately, there is often little a company can do, so be sure you really like the fabric and piece before ordering. While there are exceptions, special orders can rarely be returned.

If you return a stock item from a large retailer, they'll often accept it but charge you a restocking fee. Plus you may lose your deposit.

Q: Is it a good idea to spray upholstery with a fabric guard product?
A: Most manufacturers will offer this service, with a charge, of course. If so, resist the temptation to apply more yourself. Many times the fabric carries a guarantee. If you apply a solvent on the fabric, it may void the original guarantee. So if you spill something, and it doesn't come out, you'll have to live with the stain.

reupholstering
chairs

Turn an eyesore into an elegant accent. Consider these ideas before tossing out that outdated chair. You'll be amazed at the results.

t ALK to an upholsterer before heading to the furniture store. You may be surprised by the potential of pieces you already own.

Two for One

A pair of chairs with decorative details is hard to find on a furniture showroom floor—especially for less than $1,000. These hand-me-down chairs were comfortable, yet the distressed denim and tired style made them perfect candidates for a makeover.

Replacing the attached tufted back pillows with removable down ones was the first order of business. Next, the upholsterer raised the skirts for a dressier look.

To accent the inside of the kick pleat, often found on the corners of

Adding longer skirts and removing the attached pillows updated these pieces inexpensively. A 2-inch band of coordinating fabric at the bottom of the skirts adds an eye-catching detail.

before

after

chairs and sofas, he added a 2-inch band of coordinating fabric across the bottom of the skirt.

Plaids are tricky. The pattern on well-upholstered furniture should line up throughout the piece and be unbroken from top to bottom and side to side. When working with a plaid or intricate print, it's a good idea to use the best upholsterer you can afford to ensure the pattern will match properly. Ask to see some work samples. Each of these chairs took about 7 yards plus 2 yards of the coordinating fabric.

These chairs will cost anywhere from $200 to $350 to re-cover, depending on details added, structural changes, and any needed repairs. This does not include the fabric cost.

From Ruffles to Refined

Sometimes our tastes change. Luckily, so can our furniture. This botanical bedroom chair no longer fit the homeowner's sleek style.

A creamy quilted fabric now highlights the simple, clean lines of the piece. Before, the busy pattern was all you could see. Removing the skirt also altered the overall look. If the legs of your chairs are weathered, consider painting them. Most upholsterers will refinish wooden legs, but keep in mind that it will cost you.

It's the nail head trim detail, however, that really updates this piece. A combination of large and small nail heads provides a unique design. Such special details can also cost a bit more, so be sure to get an estimate.

This is the same chair, but it looks completely different without the full skirt. The rows of nail heads offer a custom touch.

This chair will also range anywhere from $200 to $350 to re-cover, excluding fabric. Reupholstering high-end furniture will save you one-third to half the cost to replace it with the same quality. Upholstering an older low-end item may cost as much or more than a comparable new piece.

before

after

slipcovering
furniture

Disguise mismatched furniture with slipcovers for a stylish, unified look.

YOU CAN TRANSFORM A TIRED SOFA into one that turns heads. Stop dreaming of the day you can afford to send that old, hand-me-down couch to the curb.

Pick the Right Fabric

This is your chance to start fresh. You'll have to decide on the room's new color scheme, how much you want to spend, and how durable this fabric will have to be to live up to your lifestyle. When Alicia Clavell was selecting a fabric to slipcover her sofa and chairs, she

Slipcover Secrets

Follow this advice for success.
- A sofa with a tight back and removable seat cushions is easiest to cover.
- Wash the fabric before sewing the slipcover to prevent future shrinkage.
- Don't rely on just a sewing pattern. Get the best fit by draping your fabric over the upholstered piece. Pin, snip, and tuck to find the right dimensions for your sofa.
- Change with the seasons. Striped or checked slipcovers offer a fresh summertime look. Warm red or chocolate brown slipcovers are cozy in winter.

had a few requirements. "I needed a fabric that was not only durable but also affordable, one that would stand the test of time, as well as a cat," says Alicia. From elegant damasks to rustic faux leathers, the materials available for slipcovers are almost endless. Neutral, cotton fabric is perhaps the safest way to go. For Alicia, inexpensive cotton duck fabric with taupe flecks proved just the thing. Its durable fibers hold up well to pets and repeated washings.

Select a Style

Slipcovers don't have to look frumpy. Their styles range from tailored to relaxed. Pick up a slipcover pattern at a fabric store, and fashion your own, or consult with a sewing workroom to develop the look that suits you best.

When decorator Jeannie Williams helped Alicia style her slipcover, they had a couple of factors to consider. Because Alicia's hand-me-down couch is a sleeper sofa, she wanted a slipcover that could be removed without much fuss. She also didn't like the idea of always having to tuck and straighten a loose cover. The solution was to combine a cover for the sofa with fitted, upholstered cushions. A series of ties made from the duck cotton fabric attached around the couch keep the cover from shifting (see below, left). The end result is a tailored look that stays in place.

Fun with Frills

Fabric sashes, large tassels, and bows will embellish a slipcover and give it flair. Accessorize with decorative pillows and a cozy throw to create a sofa you'll never again think of hiding in the basement.

left: **Renew walls with a fresh coat of paint, transform old furniture with slipcovers, and toss in colorful pillows for an entirely new look.**

above, left: **Hand-stitched ties help keep the cover from shifting and add a decorative detail.** *above, right:* **Sew pockets to the arm of your slipcover, and create a spot for storing favorite magazines.**

slipcover shopping

Many ready-made slipcovers, including designs for upholstered chairs, sofas, ottomans, and wooden side chairs, are available in a wide range of prices. A loose-fitting seersucker slipcover for a sofa will cost $80 to $130, while a tailored twill design will run $150 to $250. Both solid and print fabrics are widely available.

Fabric ties and D-rings sewn into many slipcovers make it easy to adjust the fit. Some stores offer sets of flexible plastic strips to insert into furniture crevices (between the arm and back, for example) to hold the fabric in place. (You can also use a rolled-up magazine for this purpose.) Various manufacturers, such as Sure Fit, offer coordinating accent pillows, draperies, and yardage.

You can purchase stylish slipcovers and related items from the following sources.
- Pottery Barn, www.potterybarn.com
- Bed Bath & Beyond, www.bedbathandbeyond.com
- Target, www.target.com
- Sure Fit slipcovers are available in many retail stores and at www.surefit.net.

start with a chest

Enjoy the versatility of this handsome furniture piece.

PURCHASE A WONDERFUL CHEST of drawers, and it will reward you with its good looks and timeless appeal. Whether you choose a vintage cabinet or a sleek new design, you'll gain a basic piece to use throughout your home.

Make the chest the center of a grouping simply by adding height with a tall mirror or a piece of artwork. An easy way to fill out the composition is by arranging all the main objects symmetrically. Mix a variety of items in your display, such as plates hung from wire hangers; include brackets that support your choice of decorative objects. On top of the chest, arrange lamps, books, and small accessories.

Before you buy, take time to do some research. You can learn a lot by visiting antiques shows and furniture shops to see the best pieces firsthand. Check to see that both the back of the chest and its drawers are made of solid wood. The drawers should have dovetail joints, and they should be easy to slide in and out. If you buy an old chest and the drawers tend to bind, try rubbing the sides and runners (located on the bottom of the drawers) with a bar of soap, some paraffin, or a little furniture wax. This should make them move more easily.

This old walnut chest is a country-style piece from Normandy. Space below the drawers holds large serving trays and other objects that won't easily fit in a typical chest. Antique botanical prints hang to each side, and the painted French mirror provides a vertical accent. Armchairs enlarge the arrangement, which is designed to fill the wallspace.

The chest below acquires tropical finesse from its slender legs and wooden surfaces that are carved to resemble bamboo. The cool, spare display of accessories includes a wooden tray, framed print, and a leaf cutting in a simple glass vase. The tall lamp balances the height of the mirror.

While the new wooden piece (left) has the basic proportions of a chest of drawers, it's designed to function as both server and wine cabinet. The center portion holds a recessed wine rack. Doors, detailed to resemble drawers, hide additional storage space for bottles, decanters, pitchers, and other tall items. Light distressing of the black finish gives a vintage look.

treat your windows

Your home has plenty of windows that need curtains of some sort.

1. These windows wear long, full panels that combine sheer fabric with a red print of lacy vines. Borrow this idea to make use of curtains that are too short for a new space. Or economize by combining inexpensive sheers with a more expensive fabric.

2. Swagged fabric adds height to this bath window. The treatment is long enough to cover a roller shade or a mini blind that lowers for privacy.

3. Sheer panels can be colorful, not just cream or white. This wavy cornice tops panels made longer than floor length so they can puddle.

4. You don't need full curtains to soften a window. The swag complements plaid cushions on the banquette.

FABRIC WILL WARM, soften, and enhance your windows as it adds color, texture, and maybe some pattern. Dressing a window can do everything from subduing hard lines and plain walls to eliminating a bad view. It can even make a room seem proportionally larger than it actually is. Look through the ideas on the following pages to find inspiration for your own windows.

Tricks to Try

Drapery workroom Pate-Meadows Designs of Birmingham offers some advice for using drapery panels to complete a room.

- Mount draperies a few inches below the ceiling. This technique draws your eye up, making lower ceilings feel taller. ▶

What a challenge! Here are some ideas for drapery panels and top treatments to make each one special.

3

4

for good measure

While draperies make a room, they can also break it if they don't fit. Here are some tips for getting it right.

- Be sure to measure all windows, even if they appear to be the same size. Write the dimensions down immediately, and then measure again to double-check.
- Always use a metal measuring tape. A cloth tape is too flexible to get an accurate measurement.
- When measuring for drapery panels, first determine the type of rod you're going to install. If you're using one with rings, you'll measure from the eye of the carrier ring to the floor.
- As a general rule, to determine width of drapery panels, multiply the width of the window by two or three to account for gathering the fabric.
- Determining drapery length is a personal preference. If you want the panels to touch the floor, allow about $1/2$ inch to rest on the floor for the best look. Should you want the draperies to puddle on the floor, add 6 to 18 inches to the length. To determine how much extra fabric looks best, use a bed sheet, and move it up and down until you get the desired effect. Remember, the fabric might get in the way of furniture placement and traffic flow.
- To replace existing draperies, simply measure one panel for length and width, and then multiply the width by two to get the total width for the pair.

1. Positioning panels beyond the window frame makes the view look larger. If privacy is not an issue, the panels don't even need to close across the glass.

2. Layering several treatments can create an intricate, custom look. Silk side panels, a damask-covered cornice, and a creamy sheer soften incoming light and add privacy.

3. Coordinate your room using drapery fabric to cover furniture as well as windows. Pinch-pleat draperies hang from a metal rod, and the same soft green floral covers the daybed.

4. Give importance to a small window by combining fabric elements. Here, a pleated valance hangs above cafe curtains.

• Hang treatments above a transom window rather than under it, and they won't appear to cut off the window.

• Add a funky fringe or trim to ready-made draperies to create an inexpensive yet custom look. Trims and fringes are available in a wide variety of colors and styles, so you can choose one that is formal or casual, depending on your personal preference.

• To make a small window appear wider, place panels outside the window frame.

• To re-use drapery panels that are too short, add a coordinating band of fabric to the bottom or the top to create a border. This simple addition will provide a new look without starting all over. You can also cut and re-hem drapery panels to make simple cafe curtains.

• If you want to mask an unattractive window, combine draperies with wooden blinds in a rich wood tone.

• Drapery hardware can get expensive; rods, brackets, and rings add up. Look for inexpensive alternatives to rods such as PVC pipe or electrical conduit. Paint the rod black to resemble iron, or paint it silver or gold for a dressier appearance. You could also cover a plastic pipe with fabric.

3

4

Functional: A window treatment made so that it can be opened and closed or raised and lowered to completely cover or expose a window.

Interlining: A flannel-like fabric that is sewn between the face fabric and the lining. Often used in panels, interlining adds body and gives a luxurious look to the drapery. It also helps to protect the face fabric from fading due to sun exposure.

Leading edge: The two vertical edges of the panels that meet in the center of the window. This is often where decorative trim is applied.

Puddle: The portion of a long drapery panel that is arranged on the floor.

Return: The outside edge of the panels where the fabric extends from the last pleat to the wall. This element is important in covering the sides of the brackets and preventing light gaps.

Selvage: The edge of left and right sides of fabric, often made of heavier threads to prevent raveling.

Shirr: Gathering a piece of fabric onto a rod through a rod pocket.

Stationary: Side panels consisting of fabric that is meant to be purely decorative, not functional.

Traverse rod: A rod that incorporates draw cords and a pulley system to open and close draperies.

Width of fabric: A term used to describe one width of material measured from selvage to selvage.

add
interest
to shelves
Set the stage for magnificent displays by adding color and texture to bookshelves.

above: **Green paint provides a delicious backdrop for this collection of black tole trays. The natural hue adds color without distracting from the composition.**

above: **Wallpaper makes a great option for the back of a bookcase. Often all you need is one roll. Vary the arrangement of books and other items from shelf to shelf to keep the eye moving and to create visual interest.** *left:* **Call attention to important pieces by using books to elevate plates and other decorative items.**

S TAID ROWS OF BOOKS CAN BE DULL when what you're really after is a pretty vignette. Give your arrangement extended shelf life by addressing the back wall first. With little expense and in less than a day, you can set the scene for a dramatic display.

Colorful Personality

If you long for color but want a more subtle result, opt for a natural favorite: green. Here, it is used to highlight a collection of black tole (hand-painted tinware) trays. Hint: Black and green make great partners. The look is elegant yet inexpensive. You can find trays in antiques stores, secondhand shops, and at garage sales. Pieces with weathered finishes work well for this look. Trays add a patterned background for highlighting other items. Lean the trays against the back of the bookcase, or set them on plate stands.

Even the least skillful among us

can wield a paintbrush to great effect. For shelves, paint the back in a color that coordinates with the room's decor. Because books and decorative items will cover much of the color, go for a bold hue. A Dijon

right: **A shot of color (Cork #2153-40 by Benjamin Moore Paints) enhances the display of accessories, pottery, framed photographs, and books.**

mustard yellow adds spice to this display of Asian accessories, carved candlesticks, and framed prints.

When painting the back of a bookcase, first remove the shelves. Use painter's tape to mask off the inner sides of the bookcase. Allow the paint to dry, remove the tape, and replace the shelves. Your favorite collections and books will really shine against such a delicious backdrop.

Pretty Paper

To add pattern to the back of a bookcase, opt for wallpaper (see page 58). Choose a design that coordinates with the rest of the room. Look for wallpaper that has a small repeating pattern, because larger patterns will get lost behind books and other accessories. For more texture, try lining a bookcase with fabric or grass cloth instead.

If you don't want to commit to one color or pattern, apply paint, wallpaper, or fabric to a sheet of ¼-inch cabinet-grade plywood or foam-core board, cut to fit inside the bookcase. This way, you can change out the look for different seasons.

Country Charm

For a warm and casual look, add pine paneling to the back of your bookcase. It's the ideal setting for a collection of down-to-earth knickknacks and books.

Remove the existing shelves, and measure the back of the bookcase. Attach panels edge to edge with wood glue, and position them so that the end-grain alternates from panel to panel. This keeps the wood from curving in one direction over time. To avoid the extra work of gluing separate pieces, you also can buy a sheet of cabinet-grade plywood.

With a router, create evenly spaced insets in the panels. Apply stain to

above: **Twelve-foot-tall built-ins line the walls to create a library setting. Keep seldom-used items on the upper and lower shelves.**

highlight the grain of the wood. Using a glue gun, attach lengths of rope in the insets. Slide the paneling into place, and replace the shelves.

The natural grain of the panels provides the perfect backdrop for fishing and hunting memorabilia as well as other nature-inspired accessories.

top: **When it comes to the back of your cabinets, the options are endless. Here, pine panels are a natural background for a collection of rustic treasures.** *above:* **Recessed lighting within the shelves highlights favorite items.**

glass act

GLASS SHELVES WORK BEAUTIFULLY when you want your displays to really shine. They visually disappear and allow light to pass down through them, especially when you have a light in the top of the cabinet. They also are relatively inexpensive. You can get a piece cut to your measurements for less than $25 at most glass shops. Make sure you order tempered glass for extra safety, and get the edges polished for a smooth finish. Ask how thick the glass should be. Use nothing less than 1/4-inch thickness for shelves. The longer the span of your space, the thicker the glass will need to be and the more supports you will need. Also, know what you're going to put on display. Books are much heavier than knickknacks.

decorative displays

Try these techniques for stunning arrangements in your home.

can become a bookcase for a set of petite volumes. Group a collection. There is strength in numbers, but know when to say when. If you can no longer see the table through your collection of blue-and-white china, it's time to stop collecting.

Highlight the design. Add a special lamp to shed some light on the table, or flank the grouping with a pair of lamps for added presence and visual appeal.

Create balance. Symmetry is achieved when half of a tabletop arrangement is roughly a mirror image of the other half. Set a significant accessory in the center; place objects to each side that are similar in size and shape.

Personalize it. Let your tablescape refer to your family, travels, or experiences. Add a photograph from a memorable trip, or a memento from a loved one.

Leave space for a small bud vase or planter. Fresh flowers or greenery on your tabletop will bring it to life.

Y OU MAY HAVE CLOSETS FULL OF ITEMS that are begging to be put out on display for all to see. But how do you achieve an attractive composition instead of cluttered chaos?

Look around your house, and pull items with a similar color palette or theme. Then consider these suggestions for arranging your accessories.

Examine what is hanging on the wall above your display as a part of the overall composition if your table sits against a wall. Use accessories that will enhance the artwork. Try to include one object that extends to eye level, and then place items at gradually decreasing

heights to direct attention down to the tabletop.

Stack books to create an instant pedestal for a small tureen or sugar bowl (above, right). Leather-bound books add character to the mix. Hit estate sales or thrift stores to stock up on old volumes.

Buy only things that you love or that have special meaning to you. Otherwise, you'll end up with just a bunch of stuff you'll likely tire of easily.

Vary the size and shapes of china pieces you use.

It's perfectly fine to mix pattern styles, just keep them in the same color family for a unified look. Use the proper-size plate stand. A large platter placed on top of a tiny stand spells disaster.

Mix old and new items. Add something modern to keep the arrangement fresh. Antique pieces take on a whole new look when combined with a contemporary painting (top).

Use the unusual. Think of a creative placement for an item. A small chair

bright creations

Transform a treasured item into a one-of-a-kind light fixture.

BRING A LITTLE SHINE into your home by designing your own original lamp. Use architectural elements, old vases, toys, or garden statuary as decorative bases for custom lamps. It's easier than you think.

First, find a lamp store or a repair shop in your area that can turn your prized possession into a well-finished lamp. Prices may vary a bit, but labor and parts usually run about $50. Lampshades can cost anywhere from $10

to $300 each, depending on the material you choose.

There are at least two basic methods of converting objects into lamps. If your item has a center hole large enough to contain a lamp rod, then the wiring can run through this opening. If there is no center hole and the piece (such as concrete statuary) can't be drilled for a lamp rod, then a figurine extension rod, which contains the wiring and supports the shade, will be attached to a wooden base. The object is then set on the base. ▶

garden style

For ease in moving this lamp, the heavy concrete fruit basket is not attached to the base. Felt pads prevent scratches on the base and also protect the tabletop.

terra-cotta column

This salvaged piece of terra-cotta makes an elegant lamp. The center was carefully drilled with a diamond-core bit. (Remember, when dealing with a fragile material, there's a chance that the piece will be damaged.)

ship ahoy

Docked on a wooden base, this lamp accents a child's bedroom. The rod attaches directly to the base, leaving the sailboat untouched. An octagonal linen shade provides a finishing touch.

buying other elements

- An adjustable three-way bulb socket lets you raise or lower the light level and adjust the ambience with just a turn of the switch.

- Harps (the metal frame that supports the shade) are available in several sizes and can be replaced to adjust the overall height of a lamp.

- Electric cords should be a color that will recede against the wall or floor.

- Think of the finial as the crowning touch, especially when used on a lamp placed on a low table.

interesting metalwork

A metal relic wears its original weathered finish, giving the lamp an antique look. The substantial wooden base elevates the slender piece.

PHOTOGRAPH: SYLVIA MARTIN

▲ little brown jugs

Hand-painted paper shades complement lamps made from old jugs. Drip candle wax onto the jugs, and then insert the candles into the mouths of the jars.

BASE or no base

A wooden base gives the lamp a refined look, but keep in mind that it's often not included in parts and labor; bases usually cost $20 or more. Adding one is good for fragile items or in cases where a rod would be difficult to mount. It also makes the lamp more stable.

shop for a shade

Cap your creation with just the right shade.

- For a timeless, classic look, consider shades with simple lines and proportions. All edges should be well-finished.
- Make sure the shade extends below the socket but doesn't reach the top of the base.
- Heavy parchment, linen, and silk provide a high-quality look.
- Paper shades are less expensive, but some shops offer hand-painted ones that are pricier.
- An easy way to get a custom look is to stencil a design on it, or add trim with a glue gun.
- White shades reflect the most light, while black shades add drama and give a delicate glow.
- Tan and off-white lampshades create softness, and gold-lined ones offer additional warmth.

with a drum ▶

Wooden objects with a mellow finish, such as this old drum, make wonderful lamp bases. The simple shade complements the drum's shape.

▲ a lamp for chicken feed?

An old metal chicken feeder serves as a great lamp with no wooden base required. An uncomplicated paper shade pairs well with the feeder's rustic style.

◀ simple switch

A silver vase, once hidden in a closet, now takes center stage in a dining room. Look for items you don't frequently use, and free up some closet space at the same time.

HOMEOWNERS: MARY LEIGH AND CHIP FITTS

◀ artful arrangement ▶

The antique block (left) contains delicate carving. Books elevate the base, and a rectangular shade adds distinction. A decorative statue of a child (right) looks lovely paired with silver baby rattles, drinking cups, and framed photos that echo the youthful theme.

eVERY EMPTY WALL is a blank canvas. While decorating this New Orleans home, designer Penny Francis used the tricks of her trade to highlight the home-owners' extensive collections. Find out her secrets to tastefully filling your home with art.

Buy What You Love

Nothing prompts an unwise art purchase like a bare, white wall. "It always amazes me how many people *don't* buy what they like but buy something to match a room," says Penny. Eventually you are bound to walk into a gallery and lay your eye on an art piece that speaks to you. It's best to be patient. Good design evolves, or at least looks like it did.

decorate your walls

Find the **perfect print, painting, or photograph** for every room.

"It always amazes me how many people *don't* buy wha

top: **These sculptural sconces highlight this painting and complement its shape.** *above:* **Simple frames work best for bold artwork.**

buying art 101
A beginners guide to collecting

- Research the artist before you buy. The key is investing early. Look for artists who are starting to gain fame and have a unique quality about their work. Then buy what you like.

- Befriend a reputable gallery owner. She can be your best guide to accessing the market.

- Purchase sketches or limited edition prints if the original works are out of your price range. The most valuable prints and drawings tend to be those featuring the artist's signature work or style.

- Put a painting on layaway for a year if the price tag is a little too high. The option of monthly payments makes fine art much more affordable.

- Ask the gallery owner to lend you an art piece on approval. Take it home, hang it up, and decide if it truly suits your style.

left: **You don't have to display abstract artwork the same way the gallery hung it. Many contemporary artists regularly flip their work to appreciate it from different angles.**

below, left: **When hanging art above a bureau or sofa, it is standard to leave 6 to 9 inches between the furniture and the bottom of the painting.**

below, right: **Add height to a room by arranging a group of art pieces vertically.**

they like but buy something to match a room."

PENNY FRANCIS, DESIGNER

Blend Modern with Traditional

Add a touch of the unexpected by mixing styles. "Don't think everything has to match," Penny says. "Just make sure you have a cohesive element." Go ahead and hang modern and Impressionist pieces together, but use the same color mat and frame to unify the grouping.

Perfect Presentation

Don't force the artwork to compete. "Balance the visually heavy with something light," advises Penny. If you fancy bold artwork, keep your furniture simple and paint colors neutral. Lighten up a room of antiques by placing an airy contemporary painting over the mantel. The size, scale, texture, and color of a piece should complement a room, not overpower it.

left: **Grouping four works of identical size can have the same impact of a single large work in the same area. Use matching mats and frames to help the collection function as one unit.**

focus
on art

Art provides
the **perfect finishing touch**.
Its selection and placement
are quite a personal matter,
revealing as much about
the owner as the artist.
For **some inspired uses**
of paintings, prints,
ironwork—even
tribal masks—check
out this **gallery**
of ideas.

◄ make an entrance

In the foyer, you sometimes need to make a powerful opening statement. Designer Debbi Wayman did just that by hanging this sizable abstract painting above a bench covered in crimson pillows.

Rustic elements mix with refined ones throughout the Austin, Texas, home. The dramatic painting provides a wonderful counterpoint to the stone walls and mesquite floors that account for much of the house's rugged appeal.

carve a niche ▼

Long walls, especially in major rooms, call for attention—leaving them blank is simply blah. Savvy homeowners Karen and Dru Adams thought about that in advance when building their Richmond, Virginia, home. In a hallway, they had niches built and framed with bright white molding to make their colorful artwork stand out even more.

If you're not blessed with recessed display spaces, you can still give your artwork or prints some extra pizzazz just by adding the molding (available at home-improvement stores). Paint it any color you like as long as it complements both the art and existing wall color. It's a clever, eye-catching idea that's also easy. ►

HOMEOWNERS: KAREN AND DRU ADAMS

remember outdoor rooms ▼

The presence of an exterior fireplace on the back porch of this Athens, Georgia, home makes it a popular gathering spot in many seasons. So it was essential that the surrounding area be decorated with the same care as the interior rooms. Interior designers Anne-Michelle Langlois and Elizabeth Hutcheson outfitted the area for comfortable lounging and displayed a framed iron grate as artwork above one of

the cushioned chairs. The weather-resistant piece is a great way of adding visual interest in an outdoor area. It's an idea that's easy to duplicate using one of the inexpensive cast metal grates available in garden shops and home centers.

paint outdoors ▲

Philip Morris fills his home's neutral walls, offset by lots of windows and French doors, with paintings, prints, and sculpture that remind him of trips he has made and landmarks he has seen. A dual interest in architecture and art framed his collecting and led him to commission several pieces.

The house had a set of breakfast room French doors looking right at the neighbors. Philip built a deck and wood privacy screen, and then he commissioned a designer/draftsman to paint a large piece. "He created an outdoor painting of the Tuileries Gardens—a powerful axial view to nowhere," says Philip. "We projected a historic print,

showcase collections ▼

Creating a comfortable home meant building a new house that feels distinctly old and understated, say JiJi and Larry Jonas. The couple loves to collect art on their travels and wanted to provide a simple backdrop for their collections of tribal masks, wooden horses, and fabric art. The walls of their Louisiana home are white with a tan undertone that allows the furniture and accent pieces to stand out. Numerous artifacts and works of art are showcased amid brick arches, niches, and other intriguing architectural details.

think vertically

Architect Lea Verneuille's quaint home proves that good things do come in small packages. The charming cottage, located in Fairhope, Alabama, nestles within a grove of trees and contains a little more than 1,600 square feet.

Art that's both serious and whimsical accents each room. A pair of prints displayed in the master suite, tucked away toward the back of the house, reflects Lea's interest in the history of his profession. To give the bedroom strong vertical emphasis, he's hung the tall architectural prints above the wooden headboard. With the art as the focus of the room, soft fabrics in neutral colors dress the bed. ◄

which he traced and then painted in acrylic on marine plywood." Framed in cypress and given several coats of polyurethane, Philip's garden view has weathered some, but gets only brief sunlight and should hold up well.

- Hang oversize mirrors with two hanger hooks located on either side of the frame. Two heavy-duty picture hooks (bolted to studs, when possible) should support the hangers. Wall hooks are rated based on the weight they can support, anywhere from 10 to 100 pounds. Unsure how much your mirror weighs? Rest it on a bathroom scale.
- Measure accurately to achieve a level frame.
- For extremely heavy mirrors, consider hiring a professional to install the required supports and hang the piece for you. To find an installation expert, call a frame shop or art gallery for a referral.

eye on nature ▶

Who says you can't hang a mirror outside? Re-create this look by adapting an entryway arrangement for your porch. A metal table softened with outdoor fabric sets the stage for a framed mirror. A collection of weathered accessories completes the scene.

◀ french twist

A simple mirror becomes a work of art when it is set in a frame below a decorative panel. This is called a trumeau. Here one hangs in an arrangement with complementary paintings on wood. The look is casual yet sophisticated, adding artistic flair and visual impact to a foyer.

expanded view ▶

Instead of the expected built-ins flanking a fireplace, opt for two large mirrors. They extend the view on either side of the stone fireplace, creating the illusion of doorways to another room. This is a great way to make a small room seem larger or to reflect light from the outdoors.

mirror image

Bring these ideas to your own home, and you'll soon be singing the praises of the looking glass.

a MIRROR CAN DO what a good piece of art can and more. It adds light and color to a blank space. It creates a view on a wall with no windows. It makes small rooms feel larger and large rooms feel light. Best of all, there are mirrors for every budget.

HOMEOWNER: ANNE WHITTLE

▲ warm welcome

The foyer mirror is as much about function as it is about style. You can check your hair on your way out, and visitors can do a quick once-over when they arrive. This fancy mirror commands attention.

◄ double vision

If one is nice, two can be twice that. A small round mirror breaks up the large expanse of the square mirror behind it. It adds depth and interest to this traditional scene and is so easy to achieve.

HOMEOWNERS: JIM AND CYNTHIA WILSON

ideas
for every room

Let these spaces **inspire you** with their fresh looks, practical solutions, and clever details.

YOU JUST LEARNED ABOUT buying chairs and sofas, choosing fabrics, reupholstering and slipcovering furniture, selecting window treatments, and more. Now we want to show you how to take all those great ideas and apply them to every area of your home. Whether you just want to freshen up a room using what you already have or plan to start from scratch, these enlightening examples will show you how to pull everything together with practical tips along the way.

Spruce up your foyer with a pretty table filled with treasured objects; give your living room a lift with clever furniture arrangements; bring a dull kitchen to life with painted cabinets; transform your dining room with a touch of fabric; create some bedroom bliss with soothing colors; turn your bathroom into a personal spa; and give a child's room a colorful boost. We've even included the home office so that every space in your home can be stylish and personal. Just follow along, room by room.

right: **Create a dramatic display with a large piece of art in an entry. It will get all the attention.** *below:* **A sturdy bench creates a casual spot for putting on shoes.**

AN ENTRYWAY SHOULD SET THE TONE for the entire house. Decorate sparsely, and visitors might feel a chill upon arrival. Pack it too full of furniture and loose objects, and guests may want to turn tail and flee from the clutter.

These attractive foyers function as high-traffic areas without sacrificing style. Make a grand entrance with these designer ideas.

Collections on Display

Because this space is generally used only for coming and going, it's just the place for showing off favorite finds that might get lost in more crowded rooms. Designer Lela Smith grouped some handsome items on this elaborate iron table (right). Pretty bowls can catch keys and change for each family member. Lamps provide a soft glow that is more welcoming than harsh overhead lighting.

Laid-back Luxe

If you have a large foyer, give it more function. Add a bench or hooks for hanging coats and hats. Line up baskets for children to drop off backpacks or sports equipment.

Designer Cindy Zelazny-Rodenhaver used a wooden bench from Mexico to offer seating and make a great landing pad for packages and mail (left). Against the wall under the stairs, a tall sculptural piece takes center stage, having more impact here than it would elsewhere in the home (top, left).

Color choice is important. Wallpaper and paint should coordinate with the colors used in the rooms directly off the foyer.

Items don't have to be valuable to make a great first impression, either. Pick up a well-worn bench at a secondhand store. Stash shoes, scarves, and other miscellaneous items in baskets placed underneath. A group of similar items, whatever they are, takes on added importance and presence when shown together.

Create an entrance that welcomes and **wows** your visitors.

first impressions

right: **For a narrow hall, an iron console table is just right for showcasing small collectibles. Open underneath, it doesn't overwhelm a tight spot.**

Unify a room with vaulted ceilings by painting the walls and ceiling the same color. Here, a golden yellow gives the room a warm glow.

Whether you prefer colorful, casual, or elegant, we have plenty of irresistible ideas for your living room.

for family
&friends

GETTING YOUR LIVING ROOM to look just right can be hard. After all, it is the most visible room in the house, the one that really broadcasts your style to all who enter and take a seat. To help you fine-tune your decorating skills, we offer four living rooms packed with smart ideas. Take a tour through a lofty room filled with color; a bright white, casual space; a flowing floor plan with the best lessons in furniture arranging; and a formal setting, rich with fabric. You're sure to find a way to improve your space.

LIVING ROOM one

Big Room, Bold Moves

Large rooms look best when they're filled with substantial furniture, long draperies, tall built-ins, and expansive rugs. For this living room, interior designer Betty Glaspy remodeled the homeowners' old sofa, adding an arch to the back of it for more height; then she piled on new, oversize pillows. The coffee table and the drapery rod are also large scale. "In big rooms, everything should make a statement," says Betty. That includes the walls, which is why Betty and homeowners Suzie and Michael Lyons chose a rich golden yellow for the walls and ceiling. To give the walls something extra, Betty added a custom glaze finish; the ceiling has a flat finish. Here, antique Chinese panels frame a high window, and beams give the ceiling interest.

Tips for warm-colored walls

- *Paint the walls and ceiling the same color so that the space doesn't looked chopped up.*
- *Accessorize with other warm colors such as red, brown, cream, yellow, apricot, and gold.*
- *Limit your use of white. White flowers or touches of white in a rug or fabric pattern are fine.*

LIVING ROOM two

HOMEOWNER: MONA HAJJ

Mix neutral upholstery with wood pieces. Architectural details, such as beams and posts, give the space more character.

Simply Casual

In this beachside condo, capturing a laid-back look was high on the priority list. It's not a large space, so designer Mona Hajj used a palette of cream and white on the walls, furniture, built-ins, and ceiling to make the room look larger. In rooms with low ceilings, use design details to keep them interesting. Add a ceiling fan that matches the ceiling color, or invest in beams, and paint them the same color as the walls. Finally, balance the neutrals with rich woods so that the room doesn't look stark. ▶

Tips for simple style

- *Prop art against walls or bookshelves instead of hanging it.*
- *Minimize pillows and flowers. You only need one table bouquet and a pillow or two on your sofa.*
- *Use slipcovers on furniture. If you like white or cream, select a durable but soft outdoor fabric to cover your sofa, ottoman, and chairs.*
- *Mount your TV to the wall above the fireplace.*

Open and Inviting

When you have an open floor plan, the most important decision to make is how you would like to utilize the space. Then arrange the furniture into sections based on those activities. These homeowners wanted their large, L-shaped living room to be a place to gather with friends and family, play games, entertain, watch TV, and enjoy the gorgeous views of their courtyard.

In one section, interior designer Mary Margarett Nevin arranged a pair of club chairs and a wing chair around a piano. Nearby, a square glass table can be used to play games or serve as an additional surface to set up a bar or food table during a party. Close to the windows on the other side of the living room, a sofa and chairs circle around the fireplace and television, creating a spot to relax or soak up the view.

Tips for an open living room

- *Use the same rugs to tie together the spaces. For example, choose two antique Oriental rugs with similar colors and patterns, or two sea grass rugs. Don't mix different rugs; it will make the room look choppy.*
- *To make the arrangement more intimate, set up several seating areas around a rug. Make sure the front legs of chairs and sofas rest on a large rug.*
- *Include lightweight chairs that can easily be moved around the room, so you can rearrange your furniture as needed when entertaining.*
- *Keep all the window treatments the same throughout the room—all shutters, Roman shades, or natural woven blinds, for example.*

A large L-shaped living room is divided into several seating sections, all with the amazing outdoor views in mind.

Decorating with Pattern

At first glance, this living room may seem as if it's filled with a rainbow of colors, but when you look closer, you can detect decorator Jenny Edwards's common thread of green, rosy pink, and cream. These three shades tie the room together so that different patterns—from bold florals to a subtle plaid—work well in the same space.

Choose a dominant pattern for either your walls or your furniture, not both. It helps to determine your main pattern first. In this room, for example, florals on the floor, pillows, and chair take center stage; other prints, such as the plaid curtains, are accents in the room.

A chandelier, a portrait over the mantel, and rich fabrics all contribute to the formal look. A large rug anchors the seating area. Its neutral background doesn't compete with the furniture.

Tips for a formal look

- *Choose long draperies of silk or chintz, include pinch pleats or a flowing valance, and make sure they puddle on the floor.*
- *Hang a chandelier in the center of the living room.*
- *Use at least one piece of ornate furniture, such as a French armchair or settee.*
- *Have fun with fringe—on both pillows and draperies.*

You can mix patterns such as florals and stripes. Just limit your color palette to two or three dominant shades.

cooking on all burners

Make your kitchen as decorative and distinctive as the other rooms in your home.

IN THIS SAMPLING OF KITCHENS, you'll find hand-painted cabinets with landscape scenes; an intriguing tile backsplash and a window with see-through display shelves; and an "everything" room with plenty of space to cook and dine, work and relax.

right: **Unique hand-painted touches warm the raised-panel cabinets.**
far right: **Cabinets painted with individual vignettes spice up the kitchen. Multicolored roofing slate forms the backsplash.**

This kitchen got a fresh new look without a major overhaul.

continental flair

An all-white kitchen is standard fare in many builder-spec homes because of its broad appeal, but sometimes the look can be too stark. Ask Pat and Jane Bolin. They lived with plain white for more than 10 years before beginning a makeover. Over time, you may want to do something different that more accurately reflects your personality and taste.

Happy with the original layout of the kitchen and the appliances, the Bolins decided to splurge on bluestone countertops and a custom paint finish for the cabinet-work. They used all of their existing cabinets. For a custom look, they added a plate rack by cutting out the bottom of a cabinet and modified another to house the microwave.

Decorative artist Reg Land painted the cabinets in a style that gave them warmth and old-world flavor. "Although the kitchen is large, there isn't a lot of wall space, so we put the art on the cabinets," says interior designer Cindy Zelazny-Rodenhaver.

A Different Island

Because a painted island might be too much of a good thing, knotty pine forms the base of the new island. Its decorative legs serve a more utilitarian purpose: One is hollowed out to run electricity to the island so that the cord doesn't show. It's just one more clever idea in a kitchen full of them.

▶

The lightly stained wood on the island sets the handsome cabinetry apart from the rest of the kitchen.

Lights in glass-front wall cabinets show off teapots and other distinctive pieces. Wicker baskets offer a nice counterpoint to wooden built-ins.

chef's haven

This traditional kitchen shows an appreciation for quality and lasting design in its fine construction and craftsmanship.

Decorative Details

A beautiful ceramic tile backsplash defines the palette of the kitchen and its adjoining breakfast area. Both feature heart-pine ceiling beams and sage walls. Top-of-the-line appliances, a fantastic cabinet system, and a multifunctional island are a dream come true. Comfortable chairs upholstered in plaid repeat the colors in the backsplash.

Wood Works

Cabinetry and quartz stone countertops surround the space. Disguised by panels, the refrigerator resembles a large, built-in cabinet. Beside it, open shelves placed in front of casement windows provide display for cookware and a collection of vases. Handsome wood brackets support the shelves.

Island Dining

An ample island occupies the center of the room and makes food preparation a pleasure. Comfortable stools slip under the breakfast bar. Made of distressed cherry, the island resembles a freestanding furniture piece. To emphasize its uniqueness, Michael Steiner and fellow designer Tim Schelfe used a darker stone countertop than found elsewhere in the kitchen.

The intricate tile backsplash echoes colors used in the dining area.

▶

above: **Flanking the fireplace, French-style wing chairs add a relaxing feel to the room.** *right:* **A drop-leaf table in front of the island makes a cozy dinner-for-two spot. It also helps divide the area for different uses.**

a working kitchen

With all the multitasking we do these days, it seems only appropriate to create a place that makes life a little easier. In this kitchen, there is room to prepare a meal and eat it, to write a letter, and to relax. Designer Susan Arnold helped make this functional space beautiful as well.

On one end of the room sits an L-shaped kitchen with a center island, and on the other stands a cozy fireplace. Vaulted ceilings make this ample-size room appear even larger. The windows, doors, beams, and cabinets are all stained a warm brown, while the island is painted matte black and topped with a butcher-block surface. On the other base cabinets, black granite countertops provide durable work surfaces.

Just the Right Table
A small drop-leaf table placed right in front of the island can be easily converted into a larger table when needed.

Paired with a couple of French chairs, it makes a convenient dining spot for two. Plus, when the grandchildren are in town, it becomes their play area. While the adults are preparing meals, they can also keep an eye on the children.

An antique writing desk and chair make up a small work area. Using the same kind of French dining chair at the desk is a practical solution, because it can be moved easily to the drop-leaf table for additional seating.

A Spot to Unwind
French-style wing chairs flank the fireplace. Upholstered in a hunting-theme fabric, they reflect the homeowners' love for the outdoors. The oversize proportions are great

for relaxing by the fire and keeping the nearby cook company. A large wall basket, filled with dried wheat straw and paired with rooster prints, hangs above the mantel.

A Room with a View

Simple pinch-pleat draperies hung from iron rods keep window treatments to a minimum. The window above the sink and the French doors feature cafe curtain-style draperies. Covering three-quarters of the window, they allow the sun to filter in but still offer some privacy. The fabric injects a burst of red in the room, enhancing the rich colors of the Oriental rugs.

left: **Set beneath a window, this writing table is a great place to catch up on correspondence.**

Four dining rooms
offer rule-breaking
inspiration.

TABLES, CHAIRS, & *charm*

INGREDIENTS FOR A SUCCESSFUL DINING ROOM

begin simply enough. Table? Check. Chairs? Check. Unfortunately, it can be easy to fall into the trap of a boring room with only those elements and no style on the menu. The good news is that the dining room is just the place to test your personal-style recipe. Here are four spaces that offer design ideas for any appetite.

DINING ROOM one

Creative and Colorful

Pull inspiration from a favorite accessory, and you're sure to end up with a wall color you love. Jane Hardin did just that in her Arkansas home. An unusual, bold green from a needlepoint pillow made three decades ago led to the citrus green in her dining room. Once you've taken one bold step, take another. Throw in violet-toned fabric, and make an impact with crisp black and white. Don't be afraid to pair unusual items. Display an interesting chair as art on the wall, and use striped candles in the chandelier.

Slip This on for Size

Transform inexpensive chairs with bold-colored slipcovers. For texture, give bare legs the slip with cloth sleeves. Like leg warmers for your chairs, the gathered fabric adds visual weight to modest bentwood chairs.

DINING ROOM *two*

Mixed and Matched for Magic

Turn up the casual factor in a formal dining room filled with a set of solemn, dark wood

furniture. Fabric is the key. Just look to Jane and Jimmy Jackson's Macon, Georgia, home for proof. Designer Mary Margarett Nevin of Atlanta added slipcovers for warmth, comfort, and visual interest. The sheer linen slipcovers dress up two Chippendale chairs. "The slipcovers highlight them without completely covering them up," Mary Margarett says.

A rug also warms up a room that is filled with wooden furniture. If you have children, choose a patterned one so that stains won't show as easily. ▶

Give the Host the Most

To distinguish a place of honor at the table, choose armchairs much like these found in the Jackson home. The upholstered chairs add heft and presence at either end of the long table. While they're bigger, they don't swallow the people sitting in them. "It's important to choose chairs that are comfortable and the right proportion. You want to sit in them and make sure they're not too deep for dining or too shallow for comfort," Mary Margarett says.

This room pulls together the essential elements of a memorable space: an ample, glossy table; ceiling-high draperies; and an antique chandelier. Distinguish wood chairs with an interesting paint finish.

DINING ROOM three

Easy Elegance

Don't let the idea of a formal dining space intimidate you. Follow the example of designer Charlotte Taylor, and create sumptuous surroundings with a few essential elements. Begin with a glossy, stained table. Add dramatic panels at the windows. Hang them near the top of the wall to enhance tall ceilings. A chandelier is a classic choice for an elegant room. Because overhead lighting just doesn't cut it for romantic meals, add sconces on the wall for mood lighting. Inject color and life with a bold arrangement of fresh flowers. You'll soon be ready to seat 10 or 12 of your closest friends at your next dinner party.

Color It Distressed

Matching chairs might disappear in a room with such a dramatic table. Let them shine with their own unique personality. A distressed paint finish distinguishes these chairs beautifully and adds a welcome note of informality to the sophisticated space. Create this look inexpensively by applying several coats of different paint colors. Once dry, sand random spots so that the various hues show through.

below: Mix and match china pieces for a laid-back look. *bottom:* Dress up wooden chairs with cushioned skirts.

Dispel the myth—dining rooms can be light and bright. Sky blue on the walls sets the tone for a blend of neutral colors and casual accessories. Intended as a solarium, the room beautifully serves as a second, more informal dining room.

DINING ROOM four

Airy Accent

Maybe the floor plan says the dining room is off the kitchen and the sunroom opens to the backyard. You don't have to follow someone else's rules. Turn a bright, windowed space into a light and comfortable dining area. That's what Darryl Carter did in this solarium. Follow the natural inspirations he used to find cues to creating your own airy entertaining zone. Choose pale blue to repeat the hues of the sky. Leave windows free of heavy draperies. Pair cream-colored chairs with a rugged table. "There is volume in simplicity," Darryl says. "It doesn't have to cost a lot of money. You have to trust your eye. It's about the personal statement."

Have Some Skirty, Flirty Fun

Add a cushioned spot to wood chairs for nights spent enjoying multicourse meals. If using a cushion alone is too casual for your dining room chairs, add a short skirt. The length brings a touch of dressiness, but, unlike a floor-length skirt, it doesn't sacrifice informal charm. Plus, it still showcases the bones of a well-crafted chair.

BEAUTIFUL BEDROOMS

Dramatic or
simple, in rich
colors or pale ones,
choose a decor
to suit yourself and
your guests.

above: **Dress up a daybed in solid
fabric with patterned pillows and
a monogram accent placed over
the headboard.**

A LUXURIOUS MASTER BEDROOM or an inviting guest room is sometimes low on the list of decorating to-dos. It's easy to neglect one's own room in favor of more public areas where family and friends gather. But this is the place where you or your guests spend a large part of the day dressing, relaxing, reading, and sleeping, so give it the attention it deserves. Whether your style is upbeat or understated, these bedrooms are sure to please with their creative color palettes, ingenious blends of fabrics, and inventive accents.

PAMPERED GUEST

Beautiful and smart decorative choices give this guest room a lot of personality.

How to Get the Look

- Paint walls a calming green and use a darker shade for the trim.
- Upholster a daybed in a rich beige, and cover with pillows in both prints and solid fabrics.
- Keep the color scheme flowing—repeat various tones of beige on armchairs, and use patterned green fabric for pillows and the window treatment.
- Pair a simple valance in a subtle print with bamboo shades for more texture.
- Highlight a solid-fabric headboard with a dramatic monogram for a graphic punch.
- Add built-ins to provide plenty of storage and to create a wide window seat. With so many cabinets and drawers, there's less need for individual furniture pieces.

Although these colors appear in small doses elsewhere in the room, they make a bold impact when used on a grouping of solid-colored pillows on the window seat.

LUXURIOUS & LIVELY

Vivid hues create a magical, romantic room.

How to Get the Look

- Choose bedding in rich jewel tones.
- Center your bed in front of a window, and hang art or other objects in the space above.
- Include deep, almost black, wood finishes to temper the bright jewel tones.
- Add balance with matching nightstands and lamps. ▶

right: **Paint the back of the headboard black to make it less noticeable when viewed from outdoors.**

SHOPPING *for* LINENS

Besides a high thread count, consider these factors.

Yarn quality: Egyptian cotton is the finest. It's often combed to strengthen the fabric and make it softer. Or it may be mercerized, which adds luster.

Touch: Labels can't tell you how something will feel against your skin, so touching samples is essential. Make sure opened packages are returnable.

Weaves: Options include plain, sateen, and jacquard weaves. They differ in feel, complexity, and price, with jacquard usually the most expensive. The choice is one of personal preference.

Finishing: Look for deep hems, mitered corners, and neat stitching throughout.

Combine green and gold to create a calming atmosphere throughout your room.

To let a bit of the outdoors in, choose linens with appliquéd or embroidered leaves, vines, or floral designs.

SOOTHING SIMPLICITY

A cozy retreat with green accents and natural touches will delight guests over and over again.

How to Get the Look

- Choose a greenish-gray shade for the walls.
- Add white linens with natural motifs such as these with stylized vine decorations.
- Incorporate subtle patterns with matelassé bedcovers in a soft green.
- Include furniture in warm wood finishes, but avoid black.
- Adorn the room with special treasures such as a collection of seashells or antique boxes.
- Pile several layers of pillows to complement the height of tall headboards.

Hang simple silk or linen panels to soften a large window while still letting in light. Chairs offer a convenient spot for putting on shoes or reading by natural light.

Place area rugs next to beds so that feet don't land on cold hardwood floors first thing in the morning.

GLAMOROUS & GOLDEN

The richness of silk envelops this master bedroom with shimmering beauty.

How to Get the Look

- Let an ornate headboard take center stage, and keep patterns and accessories to a minimum.
- Choose luxurious silk bedding and window treatments in glowing shades of gold and green.

- Add an unexpected fabric such as the dark green leather shown on these white armchairs.
- Mix and match bedside tables to add character, but keep the lamps the same for continuity.
- Highlight the wall behind the bed by accentuating the area with a subtle glaze and decorative painting.

AIRY & SERENE

This soothing bedroom proves that pale shades and lacy fabrics can look fresh and exciting.

How to Get the Look

- Choose paint or wallpaper with a yellow tint for a warm white room.
- Vary textures to enhance a seemingly monochromatic scheme—scalloped edges on linens, fringe detailing on pillows, and a subtle white-and-beige check for the Roman shades.
- Add an understated background of color with a striped or patterned rug.
- Use dark-toned furniture, such as this stately four-poster bed, to anchor the room.
- Hang window treatments on the crown molding to emphasize a room's height.
- Put flowers in clear glass containers for a pretty bedside accent.

Four-poster beds can look imposing; cozy them up with layers of plush linens.

fashion a headboard

Turn an EVERYDAY ITEM into a bed fit for a king or queen.

SURE, IF YOU'VE GOT A MATTRESS AND BOX SPRING, you've got a bed. However, the basic combination lacks a sense of personality or style. Take a look around your home, or even outside. You may have something that will make a knockout headboard. Here are a few ideas to get your creative juices flowing.

easy and upholstered

An upholstered headboard looks great in just about any setting. Success depends on the shape and the fabric you choose. The materials are relatively inexpensive; plywood, batting, and fabric are all it really takes. Of course, you'll also need the right tools to cut the wood and a staple gun to secure the fabric.

The upholstery details on the beds shown above lend a fresh, contemporary feel to the space. Such embellishments can be lost on a busy print, but they really stand out on solids.

To make your own upholstered headboard, first cut the plywood to the desired size, and sand all the edges. Cover the front and sides with high-loft polyester batting cut slightly larger than the headboard. Use a staple gun to secure the batting to the back of the plywood. Trim away excess batting. Stretch the fabric taut to cover the batting, and secure it with a staple gun. Embellish with buttons and trim for a well-finished look.

heightened headboard

Mattresses seem to be getting thicker and thicker. That additional height, plus decorative pillows, can hide a headboard. Use fabric to elevate the look (left). Simply loop fabric through a decorative bracket hung above the bed. Then tie the fabric to the corners of each headboard, and let the remainder fall to the floor.

shutter solution

Rustic exterior shutters develop a sleek appearance when framed in iron. This custom-designed piece takes advantage of the room's tall ceilings.

Re-create this look by hanging shutters directly on the wall. Paint a band around the edges to add definition and to mimic the appearance of the iron frame.

architectural fragment

Hang an ornamental element salvaged from a historic building or found at an antiques store. Attach it directly on the wall for a space-saving and stylish alternative to a headboard. The look is similar to that of an iron bed. Just be sure that you properly secure the heavy piece into the studs, otherwise you may have a rude awakening!

A dose of whimsy, color, and cleverness brings smiles to these spaces.

create children's rooms that shine

have some fun

In the room shown at right, a spring green bedside lamp covered with dragonflies inspired the color palette. Dragonflies are even hand-painted on the walls. Designer Janie Molster chose bed linens, window treatments, and pillows that coordinate with the painted furniture. The Roman shades' scalloped edge and plaid ties give them added appeal.

A bunny theme suitable for a young child is evident in the room below, but it's not overdone. It's mostly in accessories that can be changed out. The color scheme is purple, green, and blue with orange accents. The orange is a little unexpected, but it gives the room a welcome touch of whimsy. ▶

above: **This storybook room is fit for a princess. Painted pieces frame the doorway.**

right: **Strong purple walls envelop the room, along with accents of blue, green, and bits of orange. A canopy adds presence to the crib but hangs out of the way of little hands.**

HOMEOWNERS: KAREN AND DRU ADAMS

right: **This desk's carrot leg can be replaced to update the bunny-themed bedroom. Terry cloth is a soft, fun choice for the window seat cushion.**

left: **Perky Roman shades hang pretty in both the bedroom and adjoining bath. When lowered, they block out most of the sun for naptime. Hand-painted dragonflies, inspired by the bedside lamp, float on the walls.**

above: **Use a bold floral print to set the stage in a girl's room and tie all the decorative elements—wall color, furniture, and accessories—together.**

This cheerful boy's room includes a special table for a beloved train. There's room for friends to play, too.

color to stimulate

You can't miss when you put primary colors into play, especially in a little boy's room. These hues have staying power, and accessories can be updated as your child gets older. Use white accents to keep the room from looking too busy.

Here bright yellow walls wrap the room in sunshine, and bold red-and-white buffalo check comforters are paired with softer chambray bed skirts and pillow shams. Simple panels in a white-based windowpane check add pattern but not more color. Decorative accents don't need to be pricey. Inexpensive bold prints in ready-made frames make quite a statement when grouped together. The frames vary in color, but all the mats are a bright yellow to give them a unified look.

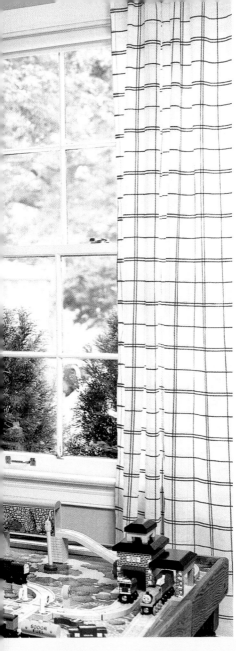

Designer Janie Molster's

Don't put too much emphasis on a theme, especially if it's very childish.

You don't need to buy a matching suite of furniture. A mix of pieces makes for a more interesting room, and you'll have more fun putting it together. You want the room to be good-looking but also practical. Use a low-loop pile carpet so that children can set up their games. Choose bedding and accessory fabrics such as chenille or denim that wear well.

Children's rooms are great places to use color. Go a little over the top, especially if the rooms are separated from the main living areas.

Paint a chalkboard directly on the wall. Here one is painted in the shape of a house and then framed with colorful trimwork.

think function too

When planning your child's room, think decorative and functional. A table and chairs serve as a play station now and as a homework spot later. A big blackboard ensures hours of fun for all ages. With a can of chalkboard paint, you can easily create an interesting shape directly on the wall. A hand-painted border makes it more like a piece of art. The one shown above picks up the colors in the rest of the room—a combination of blue and khaki that is youthful but not childish. It's a color palette you can live with for years to come.

work&play

Make your home office an **inspiring** and **comfortable** retreat with room for budding artists.

hAVE SOME FUN IN YOUR WORKSPACE. Sure, you need storage and a place to sit, but add bold fabrics, cheerful accents, and chic furnishings to inspire creativity and make bill paying a breeze. With room for children to play, you can catch up on e-mail and still feel a part of the action. Just follow these tips for no-fail style in your home office.

Use graphic patterns and bright accent colors.
Black and white always looks smart and timeless, and with red as an accent, it never feels dull. A large-scale black-and-white print fabric makes up the window treatment—a single panel that draws to one side. The animals prancing along the fabric have a childish quality, perfect for a room where little girls like to play. Give panels a sassier look with long fringe and oversize pom-pom trims.

Keep a cohesive feel by carrying the black-and-white scheme around the room. Here checkerboard tiles form a bold fireplace surround, and more black-and-white patterned fabric makes up pillows. Red shows up in a window seat cushion, on the rug, and in artwork over the mantel.

Add stylish storage and furniture.
Karen Adams, with the help of Richmond designer Janie Molster,

planned ahead for lots of built-ins and even a sink for quick wash-up after her children's art projects. Add built-ins and open shelving to your office, or use freestanding cabinets and bookcases instead. Look into all the beautiful ready-made products for storage such as linen-look and bright cardboard boxes that are too pretty not to show off.

For furniture, think functional and fun. A large desk with a whimsical

curved design gives Karen plenty of workspace. The desk is set on an angle in the room. Behind the desk, a bamboo ladder keeps magazines organized. A white table with curved legs complements the desk and is the perfect size for Karen's daughters Olivia and Sarah to work on art projects. A window seat offers a spot for anyone to curl up and read as does a comfy upholstered armchair. An ottoman that opens up for storage also makes a great addition to an office.

top, left: **Bright colors make this room appealing to children and adults.**

above: **Including a small table for children to play makes the room more versatile.**

right: **The simple white mantel highlights a vivid painting and oversize candlesticks.**

simple steps to a great bath

A little luxe goes a long way. Make a **dream-come-true** spa with these decorating ideas.

Soft aqua accents, starfish displays, and a wildflower bouquet give this Florida bath seashore charm.

beachy keen

Bring a coastal feel to your bath with these tricks.

- Open up your storage space. Use under-sink cubbies to hold all your bath bottles, soaps, towels, and more. Put them on display in dark, lined baskets that contrast nicely with light colors of cream and aqua.

- Work your bath layout around a window. Yes, this might require some remodeling, but it's well worth the investment. Natural light in a bath breathes life into a small space. If adding a window isn't an option, cheat one. Buy an old window sash at a flea market, have a mirror installed in the panes, and hang it on a wall.

- Hang only bright white towels, and pair them with a natural woven rug on the floor.

- Fill glass bowls and vases with starfish, seashells, and natural sponges. Set large pieces of coral on shelves or window ledges.

sleek and chic

Thinking outside the box when it comes to the layout of your bath can give it a totally fresh feel. So don't limit yourself only to traditional bath furniture and accessories. In this bath, designer and homeowner Cynthia Wilson refinished and painted old dental and medical cabinets for storage and hung a stained glass panel and green velvet curtains for privacy—not items you typically see in a bath catalog. That's what makes it so special. "I want to always be able to change furniture, paintings, and curtains from one room to another," says Cynthia. Read on for more of her advice for creating a stylishly serene master bath.

- In Cynthia's bath, the large claw-foot tub sits in the middle of the room, dividing the space and making it seem like two separate baths. A pedestal sink stands on either side of the tub. "I love the bathtub coming out into the room," says Cynthia. "A lot of people wouldn't do that, but I wanted to be able to face the door when in the tub."

- A pearl or metallic paint finish is a great way to add a touch of glam to a bath. "The trick is to have an undercoat that's the same or a very similar color," says Cynthia. Then apply the pearlized paint as a topcoat. Find pearlized paint at crafts stores such as Hobby Lobby or Michaels. Also, look for metallic paints at your local paint store.

- Choose cream, white, or off-white paint for the walls to brighten up a bath. Then add a dash of color somewhere in the room. "I had a stained glass window from my mother that I wanted to be the focal point," says Cynthia.

- Accessorize the bath as you would any other room. Cynthia uses a plant stand to hold bubble baths, soaps, and candles near her tub.

starring roles

Pick one element to be the showpiece in a small bath.
- Have a piece of furniture, such as an antique chest of drawers or cabinet, fitted with a sink to make a one-of-a-kind vanity. In this bath, the vanity has a distressed paint finish with a diamond pattern on the cabinet fronts. Personalize yours with a faux finish, or use stencils to dress it up. You could paint it a deep, rich color with a semigloss finish, such as charcoal gray or eggplant, and then add mirrored knobs and pulls to the drawers and cabinets for an elegant, inexpensive makeover.

above: **Going with various shades of white makes a bath look lighter, brighter, and bigger.**

right: **The stained glass window was a special gift from the homeowner's mother.**

left: **Make your vanity the main attraction in your bath. Give it a faux finish, or paint on a pattern using a stencil.**

where to find it

Charming Transformation

Pages 6-7: **Architecture** by Nancy Hayden Architect, Nashville, (615) 353-9952; **craftsman/builder** was Jim Lowe, Construction Management Services, Inc., Culleoka, Tennessee, (931) 388-4533; **custom woodwork** by Dave DesFosses, Tremont, Maine, (207) 479-3424.

Small Cottage, Big Style

Pages 8-9: **Interior design** by J. Randall Powers, Houston, (713) 524-5100.

Relaxing Retreat

Pages 10-12: **Interior design** by Shane Meder, Black Sheep Interiors, Atlanta, (404) 622-9001; **accessories** from Madison Markets, Madison, Georgia, (706) 342-8795 **(R)**, and Appointments at Five, Athens, Georgia, (706) 353-8251 **(R)**.

Find Yourself a Loft

Pages 14-15: **Architecture** by Wayland Plaster, Northwest Associates Architecture, Hickory, North Carolina, (828) 328-4902; **construction** by Kirk Boone, KCB Construction, Asheville, North Carolina, (828) 645-4628 or www.kcbconstruction.com; **kitchen banquette, dining table, and booth** built by Don Williams, Black Mountain, North Carolina, (828) 669-8666.

Explore the World of Design

Pages 16-18: To request a catalog from Wisteria, call 1-800-320-9757, or visit www.wisteria.com **(O)**.

Tropical Touches

Pages 20-21: **Interior design** by Lori Cook, Pierce and Parker Interiors, St. Simons Island, Georgia, (912) 638-3641; find **Aubusson rugs** at www.floorbiz.com or www.designbiz.com **(O)**; **brown toile** fabric is Travers Tropica (#102945) **(D)**; **ivory fabric** is Wayfarer/Straw by Pindler & Pindler, www.pindler.com **(D)**; **leopard print fabric** is Zambezi Grospoint by Brunschwig & Fils, www.brunschwig.com **(D)**; **wall color** is Desert Tan #2153-50 by Benjamin Moore Paints **(M)**.

Capture the Coastal Spirit

Pages 22-25: **Residential design** by Jim Strickland, Historical Concepts, Peachtree City, Georgia, (770) 487-8041; **select furniture and accessories** from Lovelace Interiors, Watercolor, Florida, (850) 231-9056 **(R)**, and The Studio Gallery, Grayton Beach, Florida, (850) 231-3331 **(R)**.

Red Barn Escape

Pages 30-31: **Architecture** by Tom Bauer, Bauer Askew Architecture, Nashville, (615) 726-0047; **interior design** by Mary Beth Bauer, Bauer Askew Architecture, Nashville, (615) 726-0047 or www.baueraskewarchitecture.com.

Mountain Lodge

Pages 32-34: **Interior design** by Jane B. Hodges, ASID, Side Street Interiors, Birmingham, (205) 871-0220; **builder** was Arthur Sounia, Art Sounia, LLC, Cashiers, North Carolina, (828) 226-7783; **woodwork** (mantel, bar, and cabinets flanking fireplace) by Dean Black, Blackwood Galleries, Springville, Alabama, (205) 467-7197.

Fabric Know-how

Pages 38-39: **All fabrics and trims** from King Cotton, Birmingham, (205) 322-5878 **(R)**. Cream chenille #533-58; green solid silk #275-137; green/ivory stripe silk #272-14; cotton print #213-52; gold velvet #500-06; solid green linen #491-24; printed linen #213-54; plaid moiré #270-10; gold damask #240-35; multi-colored textured weave #205-16; pink silk stripe #275-119; silk brocade #246-153; and sheer silk plaid #246-142.

Pretty Fabrics, Great Ideas

Pages 40-41: **Interior design** by Pate-Meadows Designs, Bessemer, Alabama, (205) 424-1770 or www.patemeadows.com **(R)**; **window treatment** pattern "Gusset" by Pate-Meadows Designs; order at patemeadows.com (click on "Southern Living Patterns," then "Gusset") **(O)**; **quilted velvet fabric** (Comfort Mocha) and **green tassel trim** (Oscar) from Design Finds, Dawsonville, Georgia, (706) 216-4125 **(R)**;

dining room chair fabric from Mansure & Company, Greenville, South Carolina, (864) 282-1900 **(R)**; **drapery fabric** is discontinued; **solid chair fabric** from United Textiles, Bessemer, Alabama, (205) 428-6208 **(R)**; **wall color** is Elm #TH34 from the Thoroughbred Collection by Ralph Lauren **(M)**; **drapery hardware:** Leafman Dark finials and adapters from Pate-Meadows Designs **(R)**.

Pull Color from Fabric

Pages 42-43: **Interior design** by Lori Cook, Pierce and Parker Interiors, St. Simons Island, Georgia, (912) 638-3641; **Monuments d'Egypte toile fabric** by Pierre Frey **(D)**; **solid coral fabric** is Crosshatch Woven Texture (color #603) by Brunschwig & Fils, www.brunschwig.com **(D)**; **solid ivory fabric** is Donegal Texture/Blonde by F. Schumacher & Co., www.fschumacher.com **(D)**; **checked fabric** is by Lee Jofa, www.leejofa.com **(D)**; **wall color** is Wheeling Neutral #HC-92 by Benjamin Moore Paints **(M)**.

Pick Colors from Art

Pages 44-45: **Interior design** by Mary McWilliams, Mary Mac & Company, Atlanta, (404) 816-0170 or marymac@marymacandcompany.com; **red botanical fabric** on table skirt and pillows by Cowtan & Tout **(D)**; **leaf print** used on sofa pillows is pattern 25532 by F. Schumacher & Co., www.fschumacher.com **(D)**; **animal print ottoman** is #53640.01 by Brunschwig & Fils, www.brunschwig.com **(D)**.

How to Buy a Sofa or Chair

Pages 46-47: Richard Tubb Interiors, inside Pepper Place, Birmingham, (205) 324-7613.

Reupholstering Chairs

Pages 48-49: **Plaid fabric** on chairs by

Stroheim and Romann, www.stroheim.com (D); upholstery by First Avenue Upholstery, Birmingham, (205) 591-7226 (R).

Slipcovering Furniture
Pages 50-51: **Cotton duck fabric** from King Cotton, Birmingham, (205) 322-5878 (R); **accent floral and striped fabrics** by Waverly (M); **wall color** is Summer Suede by Olympic (M); **accent paint** is Cedar Chest by Olympic (M).

Decorative Displays
Pages: 62-63: **Accessories** from A Little English, Memphis, (901) 682-2205 (R).

Decorate Your Walls
Pages 68-71: **Interior design** by Penny Francis, Eclectic Home, New Orleans, (504) 866-6654.

Focus on Art
Pages 72-75: **(Think Vertically) architecture** by Lea Verneuille, Walcott, Adams, Verneuille Architects, Fairhope, Alabama, (251) 928-6041.

Mirror Image
Pages 76-77: **(Eye on Nature and Warm Welcome) Mirrors and accessories** from Planters Exchange, St. Simons Island, Georgia, (912) 638-9888 (R); **(French Twist) interior design** by Cindy Zelazny-Rodenhaver, Interiors, Ltd., Dallas, (214) 373-1031; **(Expanded View) architecture** by Mark Carlson, AIA, Cornerstone Group Architects, Austin, Texas, (512) 329-0007; **(Double Vision) architecture** by Carson Looney, FAIA, Looney Ricks Kiss Architects, Inc., Memphis, (901) 521-1440; **interior design** by Mary Solomon, Mary E. Solomon Interiors, Tallahassee, Florida, (850) 894-1186.

First Impressions
Pages 80-81: **(Collections on Display) Interior design** by Lela Smith, A Little English, Memphis, (901) 682-2205; **(Laid-back Luxe) interior design** by Cindy Zelazny-Rodenhaver, Interiors, Ltd., Dallas, (214) 373-1031.

For Family & Friends
Pages 82-85: **(Big Room, Bold Moves) Interior design** by Betty Glaspy, Ennis, Texas, (972) 878-6868; **(Simply Casual) interior design** by Mona Hajj, Baltimore, Maryland,

(410) 234-0091; **(Open and Inviting) interior design** by Mary Margarett Nevin, Nevin Interior Design, Atlanta, (404) 352-1127; **(Decorating With Pattern) interior decorating** by Jenny Edwards, J. Edwards Interiors, Birmingham, (205) 870-5100.

Cooking on All Burners
Pages 86-91: **(Continental Flair) Interior design** by Cindy Zelazny-Rodenhaver, Dallas, (214) 373-1031; **decorative painting** by Reg Land, Dallas, (214) 742-2333; **(Chef's Haven) interior design** by Michael Steiner, ASID, Steiner Design Interiors, Raleigh, North Carolina, (919) 782-0307; **architecture** by William (Bill) J. Allison, AIA, Allison Ramsey Architects, Inc., Asheville, North Carolina, (828) 350-1266; **builder** was Dixon/Kirby & Company, Inc., Cary, North Carolina, (919) 461-0394; **(A Working Kitchen) interior design** by Susan Arnold, Susan Arnold and Company, Tulsa, Oklahoma, (918) 584-7766.

Tables, Chairs, & Charm
Pages 92-95: **(Mixed and Matched for Magic) Interior design** by Mary Margarett Nevin, Nevin Interior Design, Atlanta, (404) 352-1127; **slipcover fabric** is Emporia in Natural by Fabricut, www.fabricut.com (D); **armchair fabric** by Brunschwig & Fils, www.brunschwig.com (D); **(Easy Elegance) interior design** by Charlotte Taylor, Notable Accents, Dallas, (214) 369-5525; **(Airy Accent) interior design** by Darryl Carter, Inc., Washington, D.C., (202) 234-5926; **wall color** is Woodlawn Blue #HC-147 (flat finish) by Benjamin Moore Paints (M).

Beautiful Bedrooms
Pages 96-99: **(Pampered Guest) All paint** by Sherwin-Williams (M): wall color is Fen #8118; trim is Oak Moss #6180; **daybed upholstery fabric** is Paolo in sand by Robert Allen (D); **bed coverlet and skirt** by www.ballarddesigns.com (O); **armchairs** from Broyhill, www.broyhillfurn.com (M); **(Luxurious & Lively) all paint** by Sherwin-Williams (M): wall color is O'Olong #8131; trim is Alumina #8004; **bed and wardrobe** from Broyhill (M); **bedding and select accessories** from Jane Seymour St. Catherine's Court Collection (M); **(Soothing Simplicity) all paint** by Farrow & Ball (M): wall color is Light Gray; trim is Slipper Satin; **headboards and bedside chest** from Tommy Bahama Island Tropics, Lexington Home

Brands (M); **bedding** from Tommy Bahama Fine Island Linens (M); **(Glamorous & Golden) all paint** by Sherwin-Williams (M): wall color is Warm Patina #1401; trim is Honey White #1396; **bedding fabric** by Fabricut, www.fabricut.com (D); **headboard** from David Collum Interiors, Boerne, Texas, (830) 816-6415 (D); **(Airy & Serene) wallpaper** is Drag Light Cord by Farrow & Ball (D); **furniture** from Tommy Bahama by Lexington Home Brands (M); **bedding** from Tommy Bahama Fine Island Linens (M).

Create Children's Rooms That Shine
Pages 102-105: **(Have Some Fun) Furniture** by Posh Tots, toll-free 1-866-767-4868 or www.poshtots.com (O); **interior design** by Janie Molster Design, Richmond, Virginia, (804) 282-0938; **pink floral fabric** by Seabrook #DG3117F (D); **(Think Function Too) interior design** by Mary Solomon, Mary E. Solomon Interiors, Tallahassee, Florida, (850) 894-1186; **wall color** is Decatur Buff #HC-38 by Benjamin Moore Paints (M); **furniture** by Broyhill, www.broyhillfurn.com (M).

Work & Play
Pages 106-107: **Interior design** by Janie Molster Designs, Richmond, Virginia, (804) 282-0938; **table and chair set** from Posh Tots, toll-free 1-866-767-4868 or www.poshtots.com (O).

Simple Steps to a Great Bath
Pages 108-109: **(Sleek and Chic) Interior design** by Cindy Zelazny-Rodenhaver, Interiors, Ltd., Dallas, (214) 373-1031.

Following Fashion
Page 112: **Tole lamp and seashells** from Henhouse Antiques, Birmingham, (205) 918-0505 (R); **pillows** from Pottery Barn, www.potterybarn.com (R); **place mat and starfish** from Table Matters, Birmingham, (205) 879-0125 (R).

following fashion

Refresh your rooms with touches of a trendy color.

A rustic painted tray holds contemporary glassware in the same color family.

A tole lamp and metal container continue the color theme.

AQUA, TURQUOISE, AND LIGHT blue-green make stylish choices for clothing and jewelry and translate beautifully into home furnishings as well. Bold and unusual colors such as these work best in small doses. For added emphasis, feature them in a neutral setting, such as this gray-green screened porch.

Reflect hints of this palette in lamps, glassware, and other accents. If this cool and calming hue that's borrowed from the sea and sky isn't your style, you might select orange, kiwi, lavender, or gold. And when another color eventually emerges as the current favorite, you can easily make some quick changes.

Accessories in various shades of blue-green enliven this tranquil screened porch.